HOW TO START AND BUILD A LAW PRACTICE

Second Edition

Jay G. Foonberg

American Bar Association
Law Student Division
Section of Economics of Law Practice
Standing Committee on Professional Utilization and
Career Development

Authors of the Career Series have full opportunity to express legal interpretations
and opinions. These do not reflect in any way a position of the American Bar Association, its Law Student Division, Section of Economics of Law Practice, or Standing
Committee on Professional Utilization and Career Development.

Discounts are available for books ordered in bulk. Special consideration is given to
state bars, CLE programs, and other bar-related nonprofit organizations. Inquire at
Publications Planning and Marketing, American Bar Association, 750 N. Lake Shore
Drive, Chicago, Illinois 60611.

Library of Congress Catalog Card Number 83-73456
ISBN: 0-89707-130-1

American Bar Association
750 N. Lake Shore Drive
Chicago, Illinois 60611

Produced by the ABA Press.

3 4 5 6 7 87 86 85

Contents

PART IV: GETTING CLIENTS

PART V: SETTING FEES

PART VI: MANAGING THE LAW OFFICE

PART VII: RESOURCES AND ADVICE

Preface

This book, by its nature, is money-oriented. Its purpose is to assist the new lawyer in starting and building a law practice on a firm economic basis. Do not quote the book or sections out of context.

To succeed in the practice of law over a period of years requires a deep and sincere desire to help people. If you are looking upon your license to practice law simply as a ticket to making money, or as a one-way ticket out of the ghetto or barrio, then you are making a serious mistake. I would advise you not to proceed as a lawyer. You will do better as an insurance salesman or a teacher or an engineer. If you are entering the legal profession solely to make money, you are making a serious mistake. You might get lucky and make money in a given year, but over a period of years, you won't make it.

I repeat: To succeed in the long run, the practice of law requires a deep and sincere dedication to helping people. With proper management, the economic rewards will follow the rendering of high-quality legal services.

You are about to enter into a 30- or 40-year career as a lawyer. Don't do it unless you really and sincerely want to help people.

Acknowledgments

The wheel was invented long ago. Since that time, many civilizations have independently re-invented the wheel, wasting many centuries. Some civilizations never discovered the wheel. Much time and effort could have been saved, had one civilization been able to copy others.

Many of the lessons of this book were taught to me by others. In some instances, I foolishly re-invented the wheel.

The California Association of Attorney-CPAs, assisted by the American Association of Attorney-CPAs, has sponsored the program "How to Start and Build a Law Practice" for many years. The questions of the new admittees highlighted the lack of knowledge. Several individual members of the associations, including Arnold Magasinn, David Slavitt, Irving Kellog, Richard Berger, Burton Rosky and Jerrold Kaplan, have given unselfishly of themselves over the years to put on the program. It will never be possible to adequately acknowledge their participation.

Robert P. Wilkins of Columbia, South Carolina, suggested modifications to make the book understandable in view of regional differences, for which I am grateful. Monica Bay of California and Victoria Herring of Des Moines, Iowa, and Kathy Braeman of Cleveland, Ohio, were very helpful in reviewing the first edition of this book to modify phraseology which could be perceived as sexist.

Special acknowledgments are reserved for two people. One is J. Harris Morgan of Greenville, Texas, who first inspired me to teach these materials and who himself has given consistently of himself to the profession. The second person is my wife, Lois, who lovingly and patiently has suffered my being away from home over the years presenting this program in almost every state in the Union and several foreign countries and who has commented critically on this publication.

Part I
Getting Started

Why Has This Book Been Written?

Why has this book been written? It has been written because there is a need for it. I have spoken to and worked with tens of thousands of new admittees throughout the United States over the last decade. I know that the new lawyer needs and wants this information, and the information in this book cannot be found in any other single book. To get the information in this book, one would have to comb hundreds of periodicals and publications to get the raw information which would then have to be distilled, and unfortunately, the new lawyer doesn't know which raw information is needed nor how to distill it.

Law schools are turning out about twice as many lawyers as the nation needs. Simultaneously nonlawyers working under the general supervision of lawyers are doing work formerly done by lawyers. "Do-it-yourself" divorce, bankruptcy and immigration enterprises are flourishing. No-fault liability insurance will have a significant effect on law practices. One-third of all small businesses fail within one year.

The lawyer who enters the economic arena of private practice in an entrepreneurial capacity must know and master the principles of this book or else be independently wealthy to survive initially and to flourish ultimately. The lawyer who heeds the lessons of the book will probably succeed. The lawyer who ignores them will float along from year to year rolling up and down from an occasional "good year" to the more common struggling years, until he learns the lessons of this book or fails completely.

With due apologies to the world of academics, I have used a "nuts-and-bolts" approach in this book. Until recently, the law schools have not taught the materials in this book. Whether the reason is lack of qualified instructors or some other reason is immaterial. The end result is that at the present time most law schools don't teach these materials and this book is necessary.

For example, I have entitled one part of the book "Setting Fees" and have drawn upon empiric observations of my practice. In an academic setting, I might have done two or three years of research with surveys and two or three grants to end up with a chapter entitled "Socio-Economic Factors Considered by Providers of Professional Legal Services in Relation to the Socio-Economic Resources of Recipients of Professional Legal Services as Correlated to the Intricacies and Time Demand Factors Inherent in the Services Provided." I trust that the reader will appreciate this alternative "nuts-and-bolts" approach.

One of the beneficial offshoots of "Watergate" is the response of the law schools with respect to legal ethics. In 1970, when I first started participating in teaching new admittees "How to Start and Build a Law Practice," about 10 percent of the new admittees knew what a trust account was. In January of 1975, at the height of the Watergate disciplinary publicity, almost one-half of the new admittees knew what a trust account was. In 1983, when the State Bar of California implemented mandatory trust account procedures, less than one-third of the lawyers had complied. Among new admittees, however, about 80 percent knew what a trust account was. I personally would expect 100 percent of new admittees to know and understand trust accounts, but accept that 80 percent is better than 10 percent. I believe the 1976 disclosure of these statistics has prompted law schools to spend 40 minutes out of a three-year curriculum on this important subject, and to include trust accounts in the bar exams.

The individual chapters of this book appear to be unconnected or not in sequence. This is intentional. In most cases each chapter is intended to stand on its own without reference to other chapters. I have done this so the new admittee can most easily find the general information needed. This results in some blank spaces which may be aesthetically unsettling but which simplify use of the book.

A number of times in this book I refer to the Code of Professional Responsibility and the Rules of Professional Conduct. Every law student and lawyer should have copies of these important documents. Information on what they are and where they can be obtained can be found on page 231.

Should You Start
Your Own Practice?
(You Can Do It)

Lawyers who start their own law practices usually fall into one or both of two categories:

A. They have to.

B. They want to.

Lawyers Who Have to Start Their Own Practices

Frankly, I expect that many, if not most, of the new lawyers who start their own practices today have no choice. They would prefer to get jobs, but can't for various reasons, including:

1. They are in the 95% of a law school class who are not in the top 5% of the class.

2. They don't have a rich relative who can pressure a law firm to put a son or daughter on the payroll or risk losing the family's company as a client to the law firm that hires the son or daughter.

3. Neither they nor their parents belong to the "right" clubs or churches.

4. They didn't attend the "right" colleges or law schools.

5. They buy their clothes "off the rack" rather than having them custom-tailor-made and therefore wouldn't have the proper appearance with clients.

6. They lead a lifestyle that doesn't fit in with firm images.

7. Their wives or husbands just aren't the "type" to be social with partners' spouses.

8. They are the "wrong" (or right) color or were born to the wrong (or right) parents.

All of the above may or may not be valid reasons for being denied employment. I submit that *none* of the above reasons has the slightest correlation to success or failure as a practicing lawyer. (I expect those persons who satisfy all or part of the above list of requirements to disagree.)

Many of the people reading this book simply can't get jobs as lawyers to use their legal training so they must either start their own practice or leave the field of law. *This is a perfectly valid reason to start your own law practice.*

Lawyers Who Want to Start Their Own Practices

I opened my own doors right out of law school. To satisfy your curiosity I will tell you that I turned down several unsolicited job offers and walked away from a successful CPA practice to open my doors.

A classmate of mine went to work for a firm. My classmate told me, "Jay, you're crazy. You'll be worrying about getting clients and overhead and collecting fees, while I'm getting my paycheck. It will take you years to make up the difference between your earnings and my paycheck. At the end of five years, with luck, you'll be a partner in a good firm and so will I. You're doing it the hard way."

To some extent he was right and to a great extent he was wrong. Let me list some of the factors with pros and cons:

1. *Personality.* I couldn't take three months to two years in law libraries doing the scutwork of other lawyers, while I was being looked at with a magnifying glass for fear I might say or do something to embarrass the firm. When I believe another lawyer is wrong on the law I tell that person so (*after* documenting my position). I didn't want candid criticism of a legal position to cost me my job.

2. *Client Contact.* Three years of law school was enough. I wanted contact with clients and the responsibility of making decisions immediately. Another year of apprenticeship held no appeal for me. I had been an "apprentice" in two different unions and an "apprentice" with a CPA firm. To me an apprenticeship seemed more a matter of getting cheap profitable labor than of improving the quality of the work done by the apprentice.

3. *Practical Training.* Law firms hire associates because there is work to be done, not because the firm is interested in teaching new lawyers. In some firms there is no formal training program and in some

others the training program is not functioning because the partners have little or no time to teach you anything. If they had that time they wouldn't need the associates. Therefore, in many, if not most, instances you'll get just as much training in the law on your own as with a firm.

4. *Money.* My friend was simultaneously right and wrong. It took me five years until my cumulative earnings as a self-employed lawyer equalled what my cumulative earnings as an employee would have been. In my fourth year of private practice I was earning more than my classmates, but I had yet to make up for the difference of the first three years.

After the fifth year I was ahead of my friends, my employed classmates, etc. I've never fallen behind either on a year-by-year basis or on a cumulative basis.

After ten years some of my classmates have weathered the selection process and are junior partners in the large prestige law firms. They still earn less than I do.

I suppose that at some point I will fall behind my classmates with the large firms when they attain senior partnership. On the other hand, I believe that those of my classmates who initially or ultimately started their own practices are earning about as much as I am.

5. *Type of Legal Work.* As a CPA I had to work on matters where I frankly didn't care for the client or type of work or what the firm was doing for the client. I didn't want the problem as a lawyer of doing work on matters or for clients for whom I had no respect simply because they had money to hire lawyers and I was a lawyer. As my own boss I have greater freedom (not absolute freedom) to turn down cases and clients when I disagree morally with the legal principle espoused by the client.

6. *Security.* Except for some civil service situations, there is no such thing as job security in legal practice. If anything, I feel more secure standing on my own two feet than being dependent on the success or failure of an organization which I cannot control.

I've seen banks fire their entire legal division to "experiment on cost savings using outside counsel." If the experiment is a failure, some vice president will shrug it off and the careers of some good lawyers who thought they had security will have been destroyed.

I've seen private law firms fire associates on a mass basis when a large client leaves.

I've seen law firms and corporations where there are two lawyers in line for every promotion. The better lawyer (better-liked lawyer may be more accurate) gets promoted and the other gets fired and the competition starts again.

No, Virginia, except for some civil service positions there is no security as a lawyer other than what you carry under your hat. Security is both relative and illusory. Slaves on plantations had pretty good job security.

7. *Fringe Benefits*. Obviously there are many other fringe benefits to being your own boss:

a. *Vacations*. Go when *you* want to go.

b. *Tax Benefits*. There are huge tax benefits in being self-employed compared to being on a job (including loss carry-forwards). These benefits, however, in the main are more significant to you after a few years in practice. At the beginning you need income, not deductions.

c. *Prestige*. A firm name with your name carries more prestige than working for another name firm.

Risks of Failure

Nothing in life is guaranteed except death, and some religions claim they can guarantee against even death. There is a substantial risk of failure in opening your own law practice. There is also an element of luck involved. This is no more or less true with a law practice than with any other activity. Marriages fail, children and parents divide, even the Penn Central went bankrupt. I would not be candid if I didn't make clear the possibility of failure.

Should You Start Your Own Practice?

Are the risks justified by the rewards? In my opinion, YES. If you will follow the lessons of this book, you'll increase the rewards and decrease the risks. Go ahead. Whether you make it or not you'll never regret having tried. The lessons of failure are more bitter than the lessons of victory, but they are valuable lessons nonetheless. Even if you don't make it you'll be a better lawyer and a better person for having tried. Considering all the pros and cons, if you care enough about opening your own practice to be reading this book, you probably have what it takes to make it and to successfully "start and build your own law practice."

How Soon Should You "Open Your Doors"?

As soon as possible. You will quickly develop a liking for the "finer things in life" such as fine cars, skiing, recreational travel, clothing, nice restaurants, spectator events such as theatre, football, basketball, etc., not to mention a good apartment or home. These fine things slowly but surely creep into your standard of living, imperceptibly raising your cost of living. It is easier to "bite the bullet" *before* developing a taste for these things than *after* you have all these personal expenses.

Should You Work on
a Job "for Experience"
Before Starting Your Practice?

Notwithstanding that you have a license to practice law and have been declared competent to practice law by your Supreme Court, you probably have some doubts about your ability to competently represent clients in court and give advice.

Working in Private Practice

I don't think that the "crutch" of six months or a year's experience will assist you that much. Your "experience" may consist of doing research or making minor court appearances or preparing lesser documents. You will have relatively little client contact in most firms. The associates or partners to whom you are assigned will have ultimately little time to spend with you discussing the case or "grading" what you turn in. Lack of supervision and review is a common complaint of new associates. If the firm had a lot of free time available to supervise and teach, it wouldn't need associates.

Except in very few firms, there is relatively little formal training.

The "experience" you are seeking usually consists of access to the firm's form files, a few minutes of advice now and then from a slightly senior associate, and even less advice from a partner.

It is my opinion that there is no great detriment in developing your own forms using form books available from the law library (see chapter on "How to Build a Good Form File"). In litigation matters, the clerks of court and other attorneys from whom you get work give you at least as much counseling as you would have gotten in a firm.

The limited amount of supervision you would receive in six months to a year on a job does not in most cases justify delaying starting your practice.

Obviously the attorney who makes a commitment of one to five years in accepting a first job is taking a great risk and should be sure such a step will really be beneficial.

Working in Civil Service

At the time of the writing of this book, attorneys in civil service were receiving pay and fringe benefits equal to or in excess of those attorneys in private practice for the first few years.

My objections to civil service as a career are twofold:

1. *Limited Range of Professional Challenge.* In some jobs one can get five years of experience in five years. In other jobs one gets the same six months' experience ten times over. Some if not many civil service positions fall into this second category.

2. *The Pay Trap.* At the end of one, two, or five years, a lawyer in civil service has earned and is usually earning more than a counterpart in private practice. One often is limited in subsequent pay increases (but not limited in title promotion) because of rules not to earn more than a supervisor, etc., etc. This results in a triangle with a small apex and a broad base. There is nowhere to go. The lawyer in private practice, however, can increase earnings without limitation.

Even though a civil service lawyer can't go much farther in compensation, there are substantial pay and fringe benefits that would be reduced in private practice. Also, having proved ability in civil service, the lawyer must now prove ability in private practice.

There are some people who definitely are well suited for some civil service careers, but I doubt that many of them would be reading this book. The job security of civil service, lack of client pressures, little or no night or weekend work, generous retirement and medical plans, all combine to make it appealing to some lawyers.

Should You Start with Another New Lawyer?

Two new, inexperienced lawyers without an established clientele starting out together are similar to the blind man carrying a legless man on his back with the latter doing the navigating for both. In theory, the combination should work. In practice, it only works on a temporary basis. Therefore, as a general rule, two new lawyers getting together will accomplish very little except to prove that two can starve to death at least twice as fast as one. I recommend against it.

On the other hand, I know from experience that many teams of inexperienced lawyers have set up practice together for noneconomic reasons such as long-term friendships. A few teams will make it. Therefore, although I generally recommend against two brand-new lawyers getting together, I'll give you some suggestions which may increase your chances of success.

1. Don't form a partnership for at least one year. A bad partnership can be financially worse than a bad marriage. Your spouse can only cost you everything you have. Your partner can cost you your future. Get together on an expense-sharing basis. Each of you can be "of counsel" to the other. For example, there could be two sets of stationery as follows:

BRAND NEW LAWYER JONES	INEXPERIENCED LAWYER SMITH
123 Main St., Anytown	123 Main St., Anytown
INEXPERIENCED LAWYER SMITH	BRAND NEW LAWYER JONES
Of Counsel	Of Counsel

Check local rules for this situation.

2. Put your expense-sharing, "of counsel" agreement in writing.

3. Pick someone who complements you rather than who merely duplicates you. Remember, you need as much exposure as possible.

a. If you have the same friends, belong to the same church and clubs, have the same interests and hobbies, then you'll make great friends but will lose one of the chief benefits of association, which is multiple exposure to clients and potential clients.

b. Unless you have some reason for trying to start a specialty practice your first day, you should associate with someone who has different legal interests. The most common example I have seen is that one is interested in "Trial Law" areas such as criminal and divorce and the other is interested in "Business Law" areas. Usually, the practice ultimately tends towards the activity of the better business-getter.

c. Be flexible and ready to change your plans. Since the practice will gravitate towards the activity of the better business-getter, the other lawyer may have to readjust career plans. The "Trial Lawyer" will have to start doing corporation formation and leases or the "Business Lawyer" will have to start getting clients bailed out of jail. If this adjustment doesn't occur, there will be a falling out when the better business-getter realizes that he or she is doing all the work and needs an associate rather than a partner.

4. Be sure your "partner" is adequately financed. You don't want to come into the office one morning and find that you are the "stuckee" on the rent, library equipment payment, payroll taxes, etc., because your good friend couldn't bear half of the burden.

5. Cover in advance the problems of split-up.

a. Telephone number. A telephone number is an exceedingly important asset to a lawyer. Whoever gets the phone number may get cases originally intended for the other.

b. Unpaid payments. Who is going to pay for what?

c. Who moves? Who stays? The office location has a small value. Clients get nervous about lawyers who keep changing address.

d. Who gets the form file?

e. Provide for arbitration of differences. Individual litigation can be expensive and bitter.

In short, if you're smart, you'll have a written agreement.

6. How about a new lawyer getting together with a lawyer with two to three years' experience? In my opinion, this makes much more sense than two new lawyers getting together. The best way to improve your bridge, your tennis or your chess is to play against someone slight-

ly better than you. The same is true in law. A new lawyer can learn a lot from a lawyer with experience, and the experienced lawyer can take advantage of the willingness of the new lawyer to follow instructions and do the work outlined. I recommend this arrangement as opposed to the two new-lawyer arrangement.

Should You Practice Another Business or Profession While Starting Your Law Practice?

If you can do so, it will probably be in your best interests financially to limit your activities to law until you are fairly well established as a lawyer. In my opinion, your second business or profession is more likely to be a brake than a booster on the development of your law practice. A few people can successfully maintain two businesses or professions with both growing profitably, but they are the exception, not the rule.

If you have another business or profession, I advise you to sell it or become as inactive as possible and devote your full time to the development of your law practice. I know from past experience that my advice will probably be ignored because you'll be afraid to give up your known income for unknown income in a new profession. Three or four years from now you'll say that I was right and you should have taken my advice earlier, but until then you'll hang on to your other practice or business out of fear.

If, on the other hand, you are earning enough from your second business or profession so that you have no immediate interest in creating a full-time law practice, then you can practice another business or profession subject to certain restrictions:

1. *Attorney-Client Privilege Problems.* You must segregate activities as a lawyer from your other activities. When a client seeks legal advice from a lawyer, there is an attorney-client privilege. When the same person seeks nonlegal assistance from the "lawyer" acting in the other, nonlegal capacity, then the attorney-client privilege does not apply. You must take care to protect the client's privilege.

2. *Malpractice Insurance Problems.* Here again you must be careful. For example, if you are both a lawyer and a CPA and you sign a gift

tax return as a CPA, your accounting professional insurance should protect you. If you sign as a lawyer, your legal professional insurance should protect you. If you don't identify your capacity, you may find that your accounting carrier will claim you're not insured because you were practicing law, and your legal carrier may claim you are not insured because you were practicing accounting. You can conjure up similar hypothetical problems for the lawyer who is also an insurance agent and gives estate planning advice, or the lawyer who is also a bank or insurance company director and advises the bank or insurance company.

3. *Advertising and Solicitation Problems.* Disciplinary Rule 2-102(E) of the Code of Professional Responsibility as adopted by some bar associations states: "A lawyer who is engaged both in the practice of law and another profession or business shall not so indicate on his letterhead, office sign, or professional card, nor shall he identify himself as a lawyer in any publication in connection with his other profession or business."

Disciplinary Rule 2-103(A) states: "A lawyer shall not recommend employment, as a private practitioner, of himself, his partner, or associate to a non-lawyer who has not sought his advice regarding employment of a lawyer."

These rules, where they are still in effect, require you to, in effect, hide your second business or profession from your legal clients, and not to recommend yourself as a lawyer when you discover legal problems.

While acting in your nonlawyer capacity, there is significant debate among reasonable people as to whether the prohibitions and restrictions on advertising and solicitation were or are for the benefit of the public or for the benefit of the established law firms who wish to eliminate open competition for clients. There is also an ongoing question as to whether the prohibitions and restrictions are themselves illegal under antitrust laws or as deprivations of the public's "right to know."

The winds of change are blowing strongly in the fields of advertising and solicitation. My personal belief has always tended toward informing the public of the qualifications and fees of a lawyer so that the public can make informed choices when selecting a lawyer. This, however, may not be the state of the law and the new attorney would be well advised to follow the dictates of DR 2-102(E) and 2-103(A) or the applicable local rules unless he or she is interested in a three-to-five-year battle with the organized bar and is willing to bear the expense and stigma attached to such a fight. Each of these rules, in my opinion, represents a compromise between conflicting theories and, for that reason, is worthy of respect.

4. *How to Handle Dual Businesses or Professions.*

a. Maintain two filing systems. Don't mix the legal files with the nonlegal files.

b. Maintain separate bank account systems. Don't mix legal fees with nonlegal fees.

c. Maintain separate stationery and calling cards.

d. Maintain separate billings to the client.

e. Maintain separate phone numbers.

f. If, in the course of your nonlegal representation, you discover a legal problem, bring it to the attention of the client and offer to assist the client's lawyer. Don't offer to handle the legal problem. Explain to the client that you may not have any attorney-client privilege due to having discovered the problem in your nonlegal capacity. If the client insists on your handling the problem as a lawyer, protect both yourself and the client by sending the client a letter indicating:

1. That the client is not obligated to use you due to your discovery of the problem and your willingness to cooperate with any other lawyer the client might wish to use;

2. That you will be functioning as a lawyer from that point on at your standard rate for legal fees and that from that point on there will be an attorney-client privilege.

Sole Practice v. Partnership v. Shared Office

1. A partnership can have some economic and psychological advantages over sole practice, especially for a new lawyer. The principal advantages of partnerships are:

a. Each partner can develop an expertise or specialty in specific areas of practice, relying on the other partner(s) to cover the other areas of practice.

b. Someone is earning money for you when you are sick or on a vacation (or vice versa).

c. There is someone to "watch the store" while you are out of the office for short or long periods of time. Your client emergencies can be temporarily handled in your absence.

d. The overhead per lawyer may be slightly less for a two- or three-lawyer partnership than for two or three lawyers practicing solely. (In my opinion this factor is greatly overrated and in itself does not justify forming a partnership.)

e. You have a "sounding board" in the office to discuss your theories or issues. You can easily get a second opinion on a case.

f. A bank loan is easier to get with two signatures.

2. Sole practice (also referred to as *solo practice*) has the following advantages and disadvantages:

a. You don't have to feel guilty about spending large amounts of time on cases that really interest you.

b. You come and go as you wish.

c. You're stuck with all the administrative tasks of running a law firm.

d. You lose the larger or complex cases you have to refer out when you don't have the expertise or personnel to handle the case.

e. Many clients equate small law practices with ability to handle only small legal matters.

f. When you do earn "the big fee," it's all yours.

3. In a shared office arrangement, you can remain a sole practitioner and still have many of the advantages of partnership in group practice. Normally you are a tenant in the suite along with the others in the suite or possibly you will simply be sharing expenses. The proximity of the other lawyers will give you the second opinion and the coverage you need plus some possible additional referral work.

In the past I was somewhat hesitant about space-sharing, but with ever-escalating costs due to inflation, I now recommend it to the lawyer who wants to be in sole practice but still have the advantages of a partnership without actually having a partnership. I specifically recommend the concept of the "Fegen Suite" (see pp. 34–35).

Part II
Getting Located

Where Is the Best Place to Open Your Office?
(From a Client-Getting Point of View)

Don't practice out of your home. Clients will not appreciate your low overhead. They'll think that you're a lawyer who can't make it. Additionally, clients don't want to be seen by your family or hear a TV set or garbage disposal.

If you really can't get an office, use the attorney conference room of the local law library or the attorney conference room of the local courthouse, or meet the client at his or her place of business. But don't use your home.

Generally, I recommend starting in a suite or area where you can get overflow work from other lawyers.

I know one lawyer who opened his office in a store on a corner by a bus stop which was a major bus transfer point and was across the street from a large phone company office. In a few months he had a very successful practice of telephone company operators and adminstrative people who had the usual amount of divorces and accident cases. By opening his office at 7 a.m., he also was able to accommodate other people on their way to work between bus transfers.

The lawyer told me that this was all planned and that he bought out the lease of a cleaners after he had concluded that the location was right.

The moral of the above story should be obvious: "Go Where the Clients Are." If you are from a community where you have a lot of friends and family, then this is where you should locate.

If you've gone away from home for college and away from home for law school and you haven't much family, then you should consider moving into an area where there will be a need for you.

As that eminent speaker on law practice management J. Harris

Morgan teaches, you should look for a community where there is only one lawyer. As the second lawyer in town you'll get the cases where there is a conflict. Obviously the same lawyer can't represent both the creditor and the debtor or the claimant and the insurance company.

When I first wrote this book I didn't know much about rural or small town practice. I went to Los Angeles High School, UCLA as an undergrad and UCLA Law School. We lived in Los Angeles because that's where the family was.

After some 200 to 300 programs in almost every state of the Union, I have learned vicariously about rural, small town, and suburban law practices. The problems are very different, but the rewards are often greater in terms of lifestyle and community life and professional growth.

A practice starts with friends, relatives and professional acquaintances. Therefore, the best place to start your career is where they are.

If no one knows you, it's going to be difficult to start your practice. In a small community you become known more quickly.

If you cannot start your practice where people know you, then find a place and make yourself known there. Being unknown can lengthen the time you need to become established.

Geographic Location Checklist

1. Where are your friends and relatives (the best place)?
2. Pick a growing rather than a decaying section of the country. Watch out for blight and decay.
3. Choose urban, rural or suburban practice. Consider possible changes in economic patterns due to escalating energy costs.
4. Analyze whether you can really be happy in a rural or small town atmosphere or in an urban atmosphere. This is a matter of your personality and background.

Quality of Life Checklist

1. *Quality of Professional Life.* What kinds of cases and clients can be gotten where you will practice?
2. *Quality of Social Life.* Do you want or need proximity to museums, symphonies, discos, or other young intellectual people?
3. *Quality of Atmosphere.* Smog and pollution or clean air and water?

4. *Quality of Recreational Life.* Do you want proximity to swimming, skiing, boating, hiking, hunting, etc.?

5. *Quality of "Home Life."* Is the area safe for your spouse and children? Will you have to be afraid to go out at night or afraid to sleep with the windows open?

6. *Quality of Economic Life.* What kind of money can you earn?

You probably have to compromise some items to obtain others. There is no right or wrong. Think about where and how you wish to spend the next 30 or 40 years of your life.

Where Should You Locate Your Office for Your First Year or Two?
(From a Cost Point of View)

I strongly recommend that for the first year or two you try to locate your office in a suite where there are as many lawyers as possible and in a building which has as many lawyers, law firms and similar suites as possible.

The other lawyers in the suite and in the building can be a source of legal fees to you.

For purposes of this book, a suite is defined to be a place where more than one lawyer practices, with the lawyers having no economic relationship with each other beyond the sharing of certain common expenses, such as reception space, library, etc.

These suites are more and more available on a commercial basis; there are now companies which set up these suites for lawyers. Even if there is not such a company, you may find in your community one or more suites where there is an assocation of lawyers, or a law firm which has excess space and wishes to rent it out.

It should be self-evident that the cost per lawyer of a law library is less when there are anywhere from 4 to 20 lawyers sharing the costs than if only one lawyer is paying for it. Additionally, such features as photocopying, receptionist, conference rooms, etc., are much less expensive when several lawyers are sharing the costs than if only one lawyer is covering them. Ask lawyers already in the suite how long they have been in the suite and what they like or dislike about the arrangement. Be careful to control your own phone number.

After you have been in practice a year or two and have gotten over the initial hump of economic survival, you can select an office that you feel fits the needs of your practice.

Additionally, you normally can rent space in suites on a month-to-month basis or with a one-year maximum lease liability. If you find that you've chosen the wrong location or you don't like the other laywers in the suite, or they don't send you the business you expect, you can cut your losses short and change location without worrying about a long lease liability.

Neighborhood/Building Checklist

1. Proximity of office to public transportation for staff and clients.
2. Proximity to eating places for client entertainment and meetings.
3. Proximity to law library.
4. Proximity to major anticipated client(s).
5. Type of practice hoped for. For personal injury, workers' compensation, and criminal law, proximity to courts and administrative hearing locations or jails may be important.
6. Proximity to other lawyers for advice and possible overflow work and library is important.
7. Will office and building be accessible for people on crutches or in wheelchairs or elderly people?

Should You Trade "Space for Services"?

The basic concept of "space for services" seems to be a good idea. A lawyer with extra space provides that space to a new lawyer in exchange for a certain number of hours per month. There are various additional services which might be involved, such as office furnishings, telephone answering, client reception, reproduction services and library use, etc. Although secretarial services could be included, they rarely are.

The lawyer with space usually guarantees specified hours of work to the new lawyer and the new lawyer promises to be available for that number of hours.

This system is very appealing to the new lawyer who is afraid to lay out cash for overhead. It is also very appealing for the established lawyer who is trading excess capacity for a part-time associate without cash outlay.

Sometimes this space-for-service arrangement is intended as a "trial marriage" before any job commitment or before any merger.

In theory, this system has mutual advantages and should be a big success. Unfortunately, space for services rarely works for reasons that I will set forth. It usually ends rather quickly with a lot of bad feelings on both sides.

Because this system rarely works, I recommend against space for services. On the other hand, if both the new lawyer and the experienced lawyer face the problems which I've set forth (and others), then perhaps you can make it work.

Typical Problems in Space for Services

1. *Are Hours Cumulative or Noncumulative?* If 20 hours per month

is the agreed number, what happens when only 18 are used? Is there a "debt" of two hours to carry over to the next month? Is reduction in services justified?

2. *Suppose New Lawyer Doesn't Want to Handle the Matter Because of Conflict in Schedules.* Typically, New Lawyer owes five hours and the last day of the month comes and New Lawyer wants to interview a prospective client and Experienced Lawyer wants New Laywer to handle a matter 70 miles out of town. Who wins this conflict?

3. *Suppose New Lawyer Doesn't Want to Handle the Matter Because of Personal Dislike of the Case or Client.* There may be good or no reason for New Lawyer not to want to handle a matter or client. Does New Lawyer have the right to say "No?"

4. *Are Hours During the Working Day?* Does New Lawyer have to go down to the jail at 3:00 a.m. on Sunday morning or meet with a client when he or she has tickets to take a new client to a Sunday football game? Is there time and a half or double time for nights and weekends?

5. *Who Is to Arbitrate Claims of Excess Time Spent?* When Experienced Lawyer says that 15 hours research was insane, unwarranted and wasted, who is to arbitrate?

6. *Is New Lawyer Obligated to Do Only Legal Work?* If there is time to burn on the last day of the month, can Experienced Lawyer use New Lawyer for tasks such as picking up personal laundry and cleaning? Experienced Lawyer will claim the right to use New Lawyer in any capacity.

Recommended Alternatives

Frankly, I feel that unless the two lawyers can work out the above problems in advance, they should avoid time-for-space arrangements. I recommend, instead, exchanging checks with no promises. New Lawyer pays a fair rental and may accept or reject work assignments as desired. Experienced Lawyer pays an agreed hourly rate (about six or seven times the Federal Minimum Wage) for work performed. If Experienced Lawyer doesn't like New Lawyer's work, the work stops. A 90-day termination period should be provided so New Lawyer can find another situation.

How Do You Get
the Best Space Arrangement?

Make Contacts to Find Space

Sources of information such as your local legal newspaper are very good; non-legal local papers are all right; local bar association journals are often helpful. A commercial broker may be a good source, if the space you require is not too small. Other lawyers can be of assistance. If there is a particular building in which you want space, try a mimeographed form letter sent or delivered to every existing tenant and building manager. This is a good source of leads on sublet space when offices move or firms break up, often creating an opportunity for reduced rent.

Determine True Rental Cost in Order to Comparison-Shop Prices

Always ask for the *net* square footage figure from the broker or landlord, and put it into the lease. Divide monthly or annual rent by net total square footage to get cost per *net* square foot, which is the only true way to measure rent cost. There can be a 20% difference between net square footage and gross square footage, due to poles, beams, corridors, window sills, ducts, stairwells, irregularly shaped premises, etc.

Consider Cheap Space in an Expensive Building

Inside, non-window space is very cheap. No one wants it. With imaginative drapes, lighting and decorating, the client won't realize that the offices are inside offices. Cost savings in rent can be very significant. Indicate that you are willing to accept inside space for price or other considerations.

What Size Office Will You Need?

How many square feet do you need for an office? Generally speaking, you'll need about 400 to 600 square feet per lawyer, as follows: Personal office, 150 to 200 square feet (smaller is OK if you have access to a conference room for client meetings). Secretarial area, 150 to 200 square feet (try to defer this for a few months, if possible). Reception area, storage, copy machine, etc., 100 to 200 square feet.

What to Negotiate and Include in Your Lease or Office Rental Agreement

1. Parking for yourself, staff and clients at fixed prices. Don't automatically accept the story that parking is a concession. Buildings often make parking a part of lease if pushed.

2. Access to office at night or on weekends. Will air conditioning, heating and lights be available at no extra cost? Is there any form of building security after hours?

3. Is there any furniture from the outgoing tenant you might have?

4. Right of first refusal on additional space in building if you expand.

5. Air conditioning and heating thermostat controls for your part of the suite.

6. Be sure electric outlets are where you need them or get landlord to move them.

7. Carpet cleaning or replacement.

8. Painting or other wall treatment—replacement or cleaning.

9. Drapes often can't be cleaned; insist on new ones.

10. A one-year term, with two one-year renewal options is best for a starting lawyer. You can stay or move after one or two years' experience.

11. Minimum maintenance such as trash removal, carpet maintenance, etc., and frequency of maintenance (daily, weekly, etc.).

12. Try to delay the effective date of start of rent for as long as possible in order to gain time for delivery of furniture, announcement printing and addressing, etc.

Practicing in a Law Suite

The law suite may be the best way for the solo practitioner or small firm (up to five or six attorneys) to reduce occupancy costs in order to cope with inflation.

By definition, a law suite is a large office where many different attorneys practice. These attorneys may be sole practitioners or they may be small firms, but they are not the tenants of the owner of the building. They are subtenants or licensees of the tenant and they share the cost of reception, conference rooms, library, and common areas through their rent charges.

I must confess that for many years I was opposed to the concept of a law suite. I valued total privacy and possession of my own library, my own receptionsist who knew all my clients by name, my own reception room, my own photocopy machine, etc. Times have changed and I have changed with them. Those luxuries were worthwhile when office rents were low and could be planned without cost-of-living increases. Today they are unwarranted luxuries. Inflation in the costs of operating law offices — especially rent, salaries, and library costs — have caused me to change my opinion. I now strongly support the concept of the law suite as a vital tool in reducing costs. I especially recommend the law suite for the attorney starting a practice alone or with a partnership.

It is only common sense that if 25 lawyers share the cost of a receptionist or photocopy machine or library, the cost would be less than 25 attorneys each paying for a receptionist and photocopy machine or library. If the cost of a receptionist increases by $100.00 due to inflation, it could cost a sole practitioner $100.00 more to have his or her own receptionist, but only $4.00 more if there were 25 attorneys sharing the burden of the increase.

In accounting terms, a law suite allows individual lawyers or groups of lawyers to amortize fixed costs over a greater amount of production.

A lawyer who occupies a 225-square-foot office (15x15) in a traditional law office arrangement will need an additional 225 to 425 square feet for secretarial area, library area, reception area, photocopy area, hallways, employees' lounge, conference room and other common areas. The law suite reduces the "common area" by spreading the costs over a large number of attorneys. The additional space drops down in amount to 125 square feet per attorney.

A law suite gives the attorney a flexibility unattainable in the traditional landlord/tenant relationship because the attorney can take additional offices or space in the suite (as available) for associates, partners, paralegals, etc. The attorney can also leave or reduce the amount of space occupied by simply giving a 30-day notice, without having to find a subtenant or worry about a lease liability or liability on library contents, etc.

As an additional benefit, you may get some overflow work or other referral work from other attorneys in the suite. Alternatively, you can refer work to the other attorneys and maintain continuing contact with both the client and the attorney in order to receive forwarding fees (as allowed by the rules of your jurisdiction).

For the new lawyer it is important to be near other lawyers who can help with advice on how to handle new cases or clients that the new lawyer is encountering for the first time. The more experienced lawyers will also be a good source of current information on fee charging and other information. This is always helpful for all lawyers but especially helpful for new lawyers.

Advantages

To recap, the principal advantages of a law suite are:

1. A greatly reduced monthly occupancy expense due to sharing of common expenses.

2. Flexibility to move out (on 30 days notice in most cases) if you find a "better deal" or want to move into another law office.

3. Flexibility to expand within the suite.

4. A known, fixed, monthly occupancy expense subject to your contract.

5. Relief from the administrative problems of maintaining a library,

hiring a receptionist, negotiating lease clauses, etc.

6. Close-by temporary secretaries and word processors available on an "as needed" basis.

7. Access to other lawyers for their help in case handling or fee setting in new matters.

8. The possibility of some overflow work and fee sharing.

Disadvantages

There are some disadvantages to law suite practices, but they are relatively minor. They should, however, be noted.

1. Inconsistency of practice mix. Another lawyer in the suite may have a PI or workers' compensation, mill-type of practice. There may consistently be mobs of people in the reception room in factory clothes with their kids because they can't afford a baby-sitter. Your tax and corporate clients may wonder what kind of practice you really have and they may feel uncomfortable in the reception room. Your clients won't be able to distinguish that these people are not clients of your firm or of you. (The reverse may also be true; i.e., your PI and workers' comp clients may feel uncomfortable with the tax and corporate clients.)

2. Receptionist indifference. The receptionist probably won't be able to offer your clients any special welcome or treatment to make them feel comfortable. The receptionist won't bring coffee, soft drinks, etc., out to your client. If your clients or any attorneys waiting to see you want to call their office, count on the receptionist coldly informing them that there are no phones available to them.

3. Access to offices at night and on weekends and holidays may be a problem due to lack of air conditioning or security procedures. This is a problem with all law offices, not just suites.

4. Books missing from the library when you need them will, from time to time, be a problem, but no more or less than the same problem in a large law firm.

5. The interior walls and hallways are bare of decoration, creating a hotel hallway feeling when going from the reception room to the individual lawyer's office.

Paul Fegen (pronounced *FEE-jin*) is the pioneer in the concept of the law suite. It is to his credit that the law suite is also known as the *Fegen Suite*. Paul and I are contemporaries. I have known him since he first began his concept in Beverly Hills, California, where his headquarters are now located. His company, Attorneys Office Management, Inc., now rents to thousands of attorneys throughout the United States. I would recommend that any attorney considering the opening or the relocation of offices contact Paul before making a move. By visiting a Fegen Suite and getting prices you'll have a rough idea of how low your cost per attorney for occupancy can be.

Part III
Getting Equipped

How Much Cash Do You Need to Start Your Practice?

Regardless of inflation, recession, boom or depression, the answer to this question remains the same: You need enough cash (or guaranteed income) to support yourself and your family for one year. In other words, assume that even though your practice grows, you will not be able to take any cash out for one year.

You should plan to have some combination of the following:

1. One year's living expenses in a savings account.

2. A working spouse with enough income to support the family for a year.

3. A bank loan of the funds to live on for a year. (This will be almost impossible to get from a bank unless you have the right co-signer or guarantor.)

4. A wealthy parent, in-law or other relative to either:
    a. lend you the money or
    b. give you the money or
    c. guarantee your bank loan.

In addition to the funds for living expenses, you will need about $3,000 to $5,000 (1984 prices) to buy and pay for the following:

1. Announcements, stationery, calling cards, postage, etc.

2. First and last month's rent (possibly, you will need first and last two months' rent).

3. Down payment on modest desk, chair, two or three client chairs and some modest decorating of your office.

4. Initial payment to telephone company for equipment, line charges, directory listings, etc.

5. Malpractice insurance.

6. Used typewriter.

I cannot emphasize strongly enough the necessity of starting with adequate capitalization for your living expenses. It is theoretically possible that you will be able to take cash out from your practice in six to nine months, but an error in calculation here can be fatal. Do not plan for only six or nine months in living expenses. It won't be enough. You'll be forced to leave your practice and get some kind of job to help support your family and this will be the death knell of your practice.

If you can keep your doors open for a year, you'll probably make it as you'll have a backlog of receivables and work-in-progress which will start producing a steady cash flow. On the other hand, if you go under after six months, you'll take clients with you, and these are the clients who would otherwise have been the foundation of your practice's growth, if you had been adequately financed.

If you open your doors, then close your doors, then open your doors again, you won't get the same clients the second time around. They will remember that you didn't make it the first time and will be afraid to trust you the second time. You will have doomed yourself to perpetual failure with your first failure.

Lawyers have gone under the first time and somehow made it the second time, but this is a rarity. The lawyer who couldn't successfully start a practice the first time probably won't be successful the second time.

If I had to choose between opening my doors immediately with only six months' living expenses, or working as a laborer for two years to have enough living expenses for a year, I would choose the latter course of conduct. As a matter of fact, I worked for accountants and as a cab driver to accumulate funds. I also had a working wife, which made it possible to save cash to start the practice.

Even though you are able to make money in your practice right away, this doesn't mean you can withdraw it. You will need cash for many purposes, including:

1. Investigators' fees for personal injury cases.
2. Court filing fees to commence litigation. Even though you may earn a large fee ultimately from a probate or divorce or personal injury matter, the fee will be received one or two years from the time you get the case started, and you need the filing fees immediately.
3. Law books are exceedingly expensive, as you will soon find out.

(See the chapter on "How to Buy Law Books.") There is no end to how much money you can spend on the bottomless pit called a law library.

It is difficult enough to succeed when you are adequately financed. It is almost impossible when you are inadequately financed.

How to Get a Rich Relative or Friend to Finance Your Start-up Costs by Offering Tax Advantages

It's hard to swallow your pride to ask a relative to lend you money for your furniture and equipment. Its no pleasure to ask a relative to guarantee a bank loan for you.

Frankly, the relative may wish to follow Polonius' well-known advice, "Neither a borrower nor a lender be." Additionally, the relative may have serious doubts about your ability to repay the loan or the bank. (You also may have these doubts.)

One way to entice your rich relative or friend to help you is to offer tax advantages as follows:

A. You select the furniture and equipment you want. List the price and where the equipment can be obtained. (You are doing the leg work.)

B. Give your list to your friend or relative.

C. Have your friend or relative buy the equipment in *their name* and deliver it to you.

D. Have your friend or relative lease the equipment to you. (You draft the lease.)

E. Your relative or friend gets the following tax advantages:

1. Investment credit tax benefits.

2. Depreciation expense benefits (technically, cost recovery).

3. The interest deduction if he or she borrows the money from a bank.

4. The ability to claim that they are in the equipment leasing business in order to deduct appropriate expenses for use of home as office; telephone expenses; auto expenses; other appropriate expenses. (The amount of these expenses to the extent they are appropriate may or may not be worth the bookkeeping and calculation time.)

5. Assuming both you and the relatives are cash basis taxpayers (you probably are), the equipment should be acquired and put into use as close as possible to December 31st and the first payment of rent by you should be some time in the following year. Under current tax law your relative gets 100 percent of the investment credit and 6 months depreciation (cost recovery) in the first year, with the rental income starting the following tax year.

You will get the appropriate experience in drafting an equipment lease and become an instant expert on the subject. Be sure to update the current tax law on such areas as:

1. Length of lease relative to equipment life (for investment credit and depreciation purposes).

2. Payment of 15 percent or whatever the then current tax law is for operating expenses.

3. Complying with UCC filing requirements as appropriate in your jurisdiction to protect the relative if things go downhill.

4. Getting a *dba* or ficticious name for the leasing company.

5. Deciding whether to expand the indicia of an active business for the leasing company with city license, sales tax number, personal property tax registration, separate employee identification number, etc.

6. Whatever you as a lawyer would do in advising a third-party client on such a transaction.

As a new lawyer you do not need deductions and investment credit. They would be wasted. On the other hand, your friend or relative will get immediate tax benefits for helping you.

Checklists of Needs
for New Law Office

Get Telephones Ready

1. Estimate number and kind of instruments needed, as well as number of lines needed by meeting with phone company marketing representative.

2. Order equipment (may be delay of 2 to 6 weeks).

3. Order installation date (may require 2 or 3 days to complete installation).

4. Get telephone number reserved in advance of opening office, so you can give it to printer for announcements, cards, and stationery before opening the office.

5. Consider microwave transmission subscription service if you will have a lot of long-distance calls.

6. Get directory publication dates for outlying or other directory listings.

7. Consider yellow page advertising.

8. Try to get low cash deposit on telephone equipment.

9. Get an answering service used by other lawyers or by doctors.

10. Don't forget eventual secretary, receptionist and client usage of your telephone.

11. Consider getting a cable address (or telex if you can afford it), if you want to attract international clients.

Order Furnishings

1. Determine if major items can be rented instead of being purchased.

2. Determine if used furnishings are available (should be about 60% of new furnishing price).

3. Read ads in local legal newspapers for used furnishings.

4. Minimum furniture for office:
   a. Picture of spouse and children for desk;
   b. Lawyer's desk — at least 6 feet wide with overhang in front and treated to protect against scratches and spills;
   c. One "judge's" chair for you. Try it out next to the desk you have selected;
   d. Two to four straight-back chairs for clients;
   e. Wastebasket to match desk;
   f. Clear floor pad for chair if office is carpeted — don't skimp on pad size, or chair will roll off edges;
   g. Floor lamp, if office is not light enough;
   h. Potted plant.

5. *Problem:* Remember that new furniture may take from two to six months to deliver.

6. Keep in mind that sub-letting an office from a law firm or other lessor may provide a completely furnished office.

7. Second telephone extension for client's usage in office.

8. Bookshelf for those books you need or want in your office.

9. Minimum furnishing for reception room:
   a. Four straight-back chairs;
   b. Magazine rack or table;
   c. Reading light for magazines;
   d. Client telephone;
   e. Bookshelf for books;
   f. Coat rack and umbrella stand.

Order Equipment

1. Determine if secretarial service can provide you with dictating equipment as part of its service.

2. Determine if equipment can be rented rather than purchased.

3. Determine if used equipment is available (should be about 60% of new equipment price).

4. Read ads in legal and local papers for used equipment and for equipment specials.

5. Minimum equipment:
   a. Secretarial desk (with return for typewriter);

b. Secretarial chair (if possible, let secretary choose own chair);

c. Small copy machine, unless one is available nearby;

d. Dictating equipment—lawyer unit, transcription unit and two portable tape recorders, one for briefcase and one for car;

e. Typewriter—Buy a used electric typewriter immediately upon opening your office. A used one should cost 30 percent to 40 percent less than a new one. Be sure it has been kept under contract. It doesn't matter what brand or model you buy so long as it's the same type face as that used by your outside secretarial service. In a rush situation you can make corrections to the work done by the secretarial service if you have the same type, and you can also bring a secretary into your office when necessary and you'll have a typewriter available. (Many new lawyers do their own typing.) During the first few months of my practice I sometimes brought the typewriter home at night and my wife typed my work to save costs of the secretarial service.

f. Word processing equipment—This requires a whole treatise. Get help from secretaries, administrators and other lawyers. Read ABA publications. Don't depend on vendors alone.

g. Accurate postage scale and postage meter. This will save you a considerable amount of money over the year.

Arrange for Supplies

Get some office supply catalogs from two or three nearby office supply stores. Open charge accounts with the stores. Ask for a discount from the list prices in the catalogs. Ask your secretary or another lawyer's secretary to make up an initial "order list" for you. In addition to stationery, equipment and furnishings, consider supplies such as staplers, paper clips, scissors, 2-hole punch, 3-hole punch, telephone message pads, rubber stamps and inking pads, scratch pads, legal pads, paper cutter, felt tip markers, staple removers, Scotch tape, desk calendars, pens and pencils, manila envelopes, Rolodex files, coffee cups and equipment, check protector, fireproof safe for wills, documents and receivable records, etc.

Should Your Office Furnishings be Lavish?

Any ten lawyers are likely to have at least thirty opinions on this subject. Perhaps there is no answer. My advice is for you to do whatever makes you feel comfortable, and whatever you personally think your clients will like. I have been in offices of lawyers who make well into six figures a year. Some offices appear to be "Early Salvation Army," and others are garish with rare and expensive furniture and works of art. I have also seen the offices of lawyers who went under and found the same discrepancies. I therefore have come to the conclusion that your office furnishings will not determine your success or failure.

I will repeat here some "maxims" that I have heard over the years and leave it to you to make your own decision.

1. In a "neighborhood practice," heavy with divorce, criminal and accident work, the prospective clients want a "successful" lawyer, and will be impressed by your success if you have garish, obviously expensive furnishings.

2. In a "neighborhood practice," heavy with divorce, criminal and accident work, the prospective clients will be frightened away if they see expensive furnishings. They will be afraid of being charged high fees, knowing that in the final analysis, their fees pay for the furnishings.

3. Business executives don't want to pay for your unnecessary overhead. They know that the quality of the furnishing is unrelated to the quality of the legal services.

4. Business executives want a successful lawyer, and they will expect high fees when they see expensive offices.

There are many, many more "maxims." Frankly, I don't believe any of them. Do whatever makes you feel comfortable.

I do recommend, however, that during your early practice you avoid buying expensive furniture for a year or two. You can anticipate several office changes during your first few years, and a piece of furniture that fits perfectly in one office may not fit at all in your next office.

Also, give serious consideration to buying used furniture. Your local legal newspaper will have ads from lawyers who learned the hard way that they no longer need the furniture they bought.

I recommend the following furniture for your office:

1. Formica-top lawyers' desk, at least six feet. Be sure the desk has an overhang in front, so that your client can come up close to the desk without banging knees.

2. One judge's chair for you.

3. Two to four straight-back clients' chairs. Remember that clients who are old or who have injured bodies have difficulty getting out of soft chairs.

4. Wastebasket to match your desk.

5. Potted plant.

Don't buy items for your desk such as memo pads, ash trays, clip holders, pen sets, desk radios, etc. You will be deluged with gifts of these items from well-meaning friends and relatives.

Diplomas, degrees, admissions to practice, etc. Your parents were very impressed with all of your certificates. Your clients won't be. They will assume that you have graduated from law school and are admitted to practice. It's not necessary to prove it to them or to reassure them. It may, however, be reassuring to you to put these on a wall in your office. If so, do the following:

1. Put them on a wall behind your desk. This will be close enough for the clients to see you have them, but far enough away that they can't see the dates.

2. Get them framed in glass, rather than sealed in plastic. I learned, to my dismay, that the fancy gold seals of the Court and university were permanently squeezed flat beyond recognition by the heat-pressure combination. If you want to preserve the lettering on the seals, get the certificates framed or at least investigate what you are doing when a relative, such as your mother, offers to pay the cost of the plaques.

Announcements, Stationery and Professional Cards, Christmas Cards and "Mailing Lists"

Stationery in General

Your stationery is a legitimate form of advertising and you should use only the very highest quality of engraved stationery. Clients, prospective clients, adverse parties, adverse attorneys and judges, etc., may never see you face to face, but they will see your stationery.

I shudder when I see the cheap heat process stationery where the ink chips off or causes the paper to stick together. I mentally downgrade, the lawyer and I suppose I also downgrade somewhat that person's client and that client's case. Whether this reaction is or is not a proper reaction is immaterial. The important thing is that you, your clients and your clients' cases may be judged in part by your stationery. So use only the highest quality. Saving money on stationery is a false economy.

It has been estimated that it costs about $6.00 in secretarial time and overhead to type a letter, fold it, put it in the envelope and carry it to the mail box for mailing, as well as getting the copy into the file, etc. The postage stamp will cost 20¢ or more, and the letter may be the only tangible manifestation of your legal work (besides your bill) that your client will ever get.

Your client will probably never throw your letters away. Your client (mentally) may be paying from a few dollars to hundreds or even thousands of dollars for the one letter from you, or for a few letters from you, embodying your sage advice.

For a lawyer to use cheap stationery, to me, is comparable to a jeweler's wrapping a fine diamond ring or watch in an old newspaper.

Legal services, like jewelry, are a relatively expensive commodity

to the consumer, and, in my opinion, should be well packaged when
sent out. Please keep in mind that I am referring in this section to your
letterhead, letterhead envelopes, billing stationery and professional
cards. I am not advocating this high-cost stationery for scratch pads,
forms or other similar materials.

You will need engraved letterhead paper, "copy" paper (stationery
identical to the letterhead with the word "copy" on it), envelopes, professional cards and statement paper. In order to save the cost of die
cutting, the printer may try to sell you an introductory "package" of
some of each of the above, using the identical die which looks like this:

BRAND NEW LAWYER
ATTORNEY AT LAW
123 Main Street — Suite A
Anytown, USA 00000

Telephone 123-4567

The die is used on all your cards and stationery except that the
telephone number is left off the return address. It is very tempting to
order this package due to what appears to be a special price. And the
printer may tell you that if you order the package you can get delivery
in ten days, but it will take four or five weeks to get a special die.
Often there is nothing "special" about the special price. It only appears special because you are ordering everything at one time instead
of ordering piecemeal at intervals. The major cost of printing is the
labor cost of set-up. Once the presses are set up, the cost of feeding
additional stock is negligible. You should keep this in mind and try
to order several stationery needs at the same time wherever possible.
In other words, if you are about to order letterhead stationery, check
all your printing needs.

My objection to the package is that it is obvious to other lawyers
that it is a package. I recommend not using the package and instead
having something prepared which makes it obvious that you are *not*
using the package.

Die Costs
Depending on local custom and law, the die the printer makes for

you may legally be your property. If so, don't be embarrassed to ask for the die if you change printers.

Time Lag in Printing

When considering opening or changing your office, remember that printers are worse than lawyers when it comes to delivering their work product. Time delays of two weeks to two months are not unusual. Asking your printer for your die to give to another printer can sometimes decrease the waiting time for an order.

Announcements

To whom you send announcements is largely a matter of local custom. See DR 2-102(A)(2) or whatever is your local equivalent. As a general rule, you can, and should, send your announcements to anyone with whom you have a pre-existing relationship. Again, the acceptable practice varies greatly from jurisdiction to jurisdiction. For a new lawyer, announcements accomplish the dual purpose of telling people that you passed the bar and where your office is. You may find a substantial delay due to printers and getting your phone numbers confirmed. Don't be concerned if the announcements don't arrive until after you've moved in. Order some extra announcements to send to people you overlooked on your first list. For a decent interval of time, you can send these overlooked people your announcement.

When people receive your announcement, they will read it and say, "That's nice." They may then put your phone number and address in a book and throw your expensive announcement immediately into the waste basket. (Except for your parents, who may frame it or put it in a scrapbook.)

I personally think you will be doing more for your friends and relatives if you include a professional card with your annoucement. The small card can be easily placed in a wallet to be available when your client needs you right away.

Announcement Mailing List

Your announcement mailing list is a valuable asset. Keep it updated with new addresses and clients. Eliminate people with whom you have no contact. Announcements to people you have not had prior contact with may be a form of improper solicitation.

Christmas Cards

Every year I send personal "Seasons's Greetings" cards to my clients. Invariably, the cards serve as a reminder to some of them to take care of some legal matter such as updating a will. A divorce lawyer told me that couples stay together during Christmas and New Year's and start divorce proceedings in January and February. If this is so, then I suppose "Season's Greetings" cards are a very good investment, as you may be reaching two potential clients.

Here again, local practice varies from jurisdiction to jurisdiction, and you should ask other lawyers what is permissible. In some areas, you cannot use a firm name on the card and in some you can.

Part IV
Getting Clients

How to Handle
Friends and Relatives

It is a fact of life that many, if not most, of the new lawyer's clients and source of clients will be friends and relatives. If the new lawyer can't be trusted by friends and relatives to handle a legal matter then who will trust him or her?

Most lawyers have unhappy experiences representing their friends and relatives, and it is usually the fault of the lawyer. No matter how hard the new lawyer works on the case, no matter how fantastic a job the new lawyer does, no matter how successful the result, friends or relatives honestly believe that they are the recipients of third-rate legal services. They honestly believe they did the new lawyer a favor by giving him or her the case "for experience." Regardless of the fee, friends or relatives think they are being overcharged.

Face reality. You had better satisfy your friends and relatives if you expect to make it as a new lawyer. They will be the source of much, if not most, of your practice your first few years.

There are several things you can do to improve your image with them:

1. Be friendly when they seek free legal advice at social events and on the telephone at night.

2. Get them into the office. Don't conduct your law practice in an atmosphere of blaring television, screaming children or orchestras at weddings. Tell them the case sounds very interesting, and if they can please come to your office, you'll be able to concentrate on their problem and get the facts down correctly. Tell them you don't like to interview clients outside the office because you can't make the notes essential for the proper handling of their case.

3. Don't reveal confidences. Go out of your way to tell the client

that you can't or won't discuss the case with your mutual friends or relatives. Tell your cousin Mary that you can't and won't discuss her case with her mother, Aunt Jane, or your mother who is Mary's aunt. Tell cousin Mary that if she wants Aunt Jane to know about the case, that she'll have to tell her because you won't. This touch of professionalism goes a long way toward solidifying the attorney-client relationship.

Early in my career, I represented some very close friends in the early stages of an adoption just before and just after the baby was born. I never told my wife. A few weeks later we went to the friends' house for a long-planned social gathering. At the party my wife found out for the first time about the new baby, and promptly let out a stream of not-too-kind comments for my not having said anything about the baby. (All the other couples had brought baby gifts and we hadn't.) The adopting parents tried to alleviate my wife's embarrassment by saying that they assumed I would tell my wife about the adoption and hadn't called her with the good news. I stated that I couldn't say anything about the new baby because I couldn't disclose a client's confidence. Over the years, I've gotten a lot of business and a lot of referrals from the people at that party and that couple. If my friends had doubts about my professionalism before this episode, the doubts were over afterward.

4. *Billing friends and relatives.* It is very important that you bill friends and relatives properly. Suppose $450 is a reasonable fee for your services, but your friend or relative only has $150 to pay you, and you are willing to take this case for $150 because:

a. You want the experience.

b. You are tired of playing solitaire in the office.

c. The phone company is threatening you about your unpaid bill.

The proper way to bill someone like a cousin is as follows:

Flaky Cousin
123 Main Street
Anytown, USA
RE: Professional Services Rendered
Cousin adv. People
Case C123456

One-half day trial in traffic court to defend charges of speeding violation of Vehicle Code Section 5976. Preparation of trial brief to exclude improperly obtained confession and attempting to exclude eye witnesses. Obtaining letter from employer asking court not to suspend driver's license.

Services rendered January 3, 7, 11 and 14, 19__.
Total Fee $450.00
Less family discount   300.00
   Balance now due and payable $150.00

Thank you.

The reason for showing the $450.00 price and $300.00 discount is to let the cousin know the value of what was received. He or she has no way of knowing your services were worth $450.00 unless you say so. A relative will think they were only worth $85.00 and you were overcharging. (Remember, they think they did you a favor by letting you get experience.)

Additionally, you want relatives and friends to refer you $450.00 cases, not $150.00 cases. If they don't know the value of the services, they'll recommend people to you telling them you only charge $150.00. Your cousin will be grateful to you for the $300.00 "discount."

In summary, friends and relatives will be the beginning of your legal practice. Treat them professionally, and they will recommend clients to you. Treat them with scorn and disdain, and your practice may never get a good start.

How to Market Your Services

Start on Announcements

1. Prepare mailing lists:
   a. Law school class (get addresses from Alumni Association);
   b. Undergraduate classmates (get addresses from Alumni Association);
   c. High school classmates, if appropriate (get addresses from Alumni Association);
   d. Church members, if appropriate;
   e. Family (your mother will be glad to help you);
   f. Organizations you belong(ed) to—sports clubs, social clubs, philanthropic clubs (get addresses from club secretary);
   g. Professional associations you belong to.
2. Get sample announcements from printer.
3. Get time and cost estimates from printer.
4. Decide on style of announcements (listing or not listing areas of practice).
5. Remember to order professional cards and enclose one with announcements.
6. Don't use cheap announcements or cards (be sure you get them engraved, on good stock).
7. Get cost and time estimate from professional addressing service for addressing, stuffing and mailing announcements.
8. Start addresssing envelopes while announcements are being printed.
9. Consider buying old postage stamps from stamp dealer for postage to attract attention to the announcement when it is received.

Order Stationery

Allow up to two months delivery time for high-quality stationery. Get a catalogue with samples from a national supplier such as Stuart Cooper, or a local company. Order letter-size bond letterhead, and second sheets. Also blank letter-sized bond, letter-sized envelopes, professional cards, announcements, Will paper and Will covers.

If your state allows or requires letter-size pleadings, don't use "contract" or "pleading size" stationery.

Also get "cheap" envelopes for bill-paying from post office. Order billing stationery and window envelopes.

Cost-Effective
Media Advertising

In this chapter, I wish to touch upon lawyer advertising as it affects the lawyer just beginning a practice.

What is in this chapter is my experience in discussing advertising with tens of thousands of lawyers all over the United States. A particular lawyer in a particular community may have contrary experiences but I believe that on balance these observations are correct.

1. *Yellow Page Advertising.* Yellow page telephone directory advertising is probably the most cost-effective advertising there is for the new lawyer, if done correctly, because the persons looking believe they need a lawyer. If done improperly, however, the cost-effectiveness is questionable.

Improper (least cost-effective or non-cost-effective) advertising is too general and tells the potential client too much. A poor advertisement might read like this:

JOHN DOE

123 Main Street		555-1234
Business law	Probate	
Family Law	Workers Compensation	
Criminal Law	Civil Trials	

FREE INITIAL CONSULTATION

The proper (cost-effective) advertising lists the principal types of case(s) you hope to get from the advertising in simple individual ads:

JOHN DOE	JOHN DOE	JOHN DOE
Drunk Driving	Divorce and	Auto Accidents
555-1212	Family Law	555-1212
	555-1212	

JOHN DOE   JOHN DOE   JOHN DOE
Will and Estates House Purchases Purchases and Sales
555-1212   555-1212   of Business
555-1212

The "one-inchers" are extremely cost-effective according to the people who use them. I haven't done any formal marketing research into specialization, but I believe that the American public wants lawyers who specialize in the kind of problem which they have. Thus the "one-incher" is cost-effective.

2. *Newspaper Advertising.* Here again there is cost-effective and non-cost-effective advertising.

Metropolitan newspapers, generally speaking, are not cost-effective. I believe that when people read the metropolitan newspaper they skim it and have no time to study or remember lawyer advertising.

Smaller newspapers, such as neighborhood papers, shopping news, and local throw-aways, are extremely cost-effective according to the reports I get. For some reason, college newspapers and newspapers in college areas are very effective. It is my personal opinion that the people who have the inclination to read this type of publication apparently have the time to read the paper or study it carefully.

It appears that in newspapers the display ad is not any more effective than the classified ad. (Again, those people who have the time to read these papers have the time to read them carefully.) It would appear that it is sufficient simply to state:

JOHN DOE
ATTORNEY AT LAW
555-1234

Frequency of Ad. Very few ads are worthwhile, however, on a one-shot basis. To be successful, almost all ads must run over a period of time. People will look for a lawyer when they need one. Therefore your ad must run continuously until there is a matching of your availability and the client's need for a lawyer.

3. *Radio Advertising.* I have no experience or history reported to me on radio advertising, so accordingly I make no suggestions. If you have any first-hand experiences, I would appreciate learning about them from you.

4. *Television Advertising.* For reasons that I don't understand, peo-

ple just don't want to believe the truth about TV lawyer advertising. I continually tell groups of lawyers my observations in the area and then immediately encounter reservations or disbelief from the lawyers in the group. When I ask if anybody can report contrary evidence no one raises a hand. When I ask who in the audience has tried TV advertising a few hands go up and then they tell me their experiences. Their experiences match the experiences of other lawyers throughout America, yet the rest of the audience still seems hostile and disbelieving.

With two possible exceptions, TV lawyer advertising is not cost-effective and should be avoided. Many lawyers have related to me that the TV advertising money they spent was totally wasted. The two exceptions are as follows:

First, sponsoring a public service television program. Recently a San Diego, California law firm spent about $8,000 to sponsor a program on PBS television. (I believe that technically the sponsorship was termed a "grant.") The TV station is well respected in the area. The newspaper accounts indicated that the sponsorship was extremely well accepted by the firm's existing conservative business and financial clients. It is not known whether this ad resulted in any new clients or work.

If I were to spend money on TV advertising I would follow the leaders and sponsor a series or a special.

Second, there is one law firm I know of which claims that TV advertising is cost-effective for developing new business. They sell what, for all intents and purposes, amounts to a franchise for a neighborhood law office and then promise to spend the investor's money on TV ads (at least they did so in the past). I am not aware of any independent verification of their claims, and I don't doubt that the investor's money was spent on TV ads, but I don't know if there is any benefit to the investing firm from a cost-effective point of view. I have my doubts about the cost-effectiveness, but I repeat the claim that at least one firm has found TV advertising worthwhile.

In summary, in my opinion, I wouldn't spend my precious dollars on TV ads when I could spend the money in yellow pages and neighborhood newspaper classifieds.

The Importance of Accepting and Returning Telephone Calls

I needed a lawyer.
I couldn't reach you.
I reached another lawyer.
I don't need you any more.

In terms of good public relations, this may be the most important chapter of this book. Unless God made you clairvoyant, you won't know in advance why people call. When Mrs. Jones calls, you don't know if she's pestering you about her complaint about the apartment owner turning off the hot water or if she is trying to reach you because her husband fell down the unlit stairwell and has two broken legs and a broken back.

Most clients feel that lawyers' telephone calls are excessively screened. Failure to maintain communications with clients is the single most common complaint to bar associations. Increasingly, lawyers are being disciplined for ignoring clients' calls and letters.

Unless you have a storefront office, most if not all of your new clients will call you before coming in. Your telephone is your life line to new clients and new matters. If you can't return a call, have your secretary or another lawyer return the call for you so you won't lose that new client who is trying to reach you.

I think it's a good public relations for you to return calls at night and on Saturdays and Sundays. Tell the client you are concerned about his or her call and didn't want to wait until the next morning or until after the weekend to return it. The client will really appreciate your concern.

Be sure you use a duplicate phone message system for *all* telephone messages to protect yourself from the client who claims to have called you ten times and you didn't return any of the calls. When you try to return the call without success, note on the message itself your efforts.

Sample notations would be:

3/1/84	10:04 a.m.	BY—	Busy
3/1/84	10:30 a.m.	BY—	Busy
3/1/84	1:00 p.m.	N/A—	No Answer
3/1/84	5:00 p.m.	N/A—	No Answer
3/2/84	9:00 a.m.	WCB—	Not in, left message will call back

You might even send the client a speed letter or form letter as follows:

Dear Client:

I tried five times to return your call of March 1st. Please call me or drop me a note so that we can help you if necessary.

Very truly yours,

John Novice

Logging Incoming Telephone Calls. I don't. Some lawyers do. If the client connects on the call, I have notes in the file and my time records to verify the call. If the client doesn't connect, I have my return message carbon copy. I've never needed a log of incoming calls. In some situations they might be worthwhile, but I doubt it.

Telephone. Telephones are your lifeline to new clients. Use a speaker phone so you can take notes during conversations and can go through files for information while talking on the phone. Get an extension phone in your office so your client can listen in. Get rotary lines. Three to four lines should be adequate during your first year. A client who gets a busy signal may call the next lawyer on the list. List yourself in as many phone books as your local ethical rules permit. Never use another lawyer's phone number. Get your own number. Clients often will take the first lawyer they can get hold of. Don't use mechanical answering devices. Use an exchange instead.

PETERS VS JONES

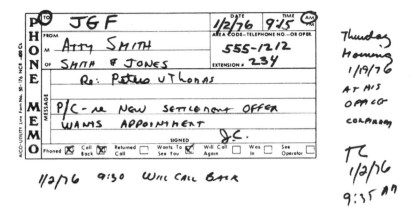

PHONE MEMO

TO: JGF
DATE 1/2/76 TIME 9:15 AM

FROM: Atty SMITH
AREA CODE—TELEPHONE NO.—OR OPER. 555-1212

OF: SMITH & JONES
EXTENSION # 234

Re: Peters v Thomas

P/C - re NEW SETTLEMENT OFFER
WANTS APPOINTMENT

SIGNED JC.

Phoned ☒ Call Back ☒ Returned Call ☐ Wants To See You ☑ Will Call Again ☐ Was In ☐ See Operator ☐

Thursday
Morning
1/19/76
AT HIS
OFFICE
CONFIRM

TC
1/2/76
9:35 AM

1/2/76   9:30   WILL CALL BACK

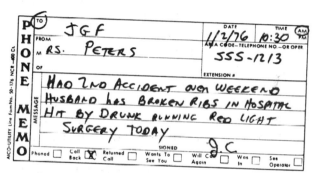

PHONE MEMO

TO: JGF
DATE 1/2/76 TIME 10:30 AM

FROM: MRS. PETERS
AREA CODE—TELEPHONE NO.—OR OPER. 555-1213

OF:
EXTENSION #

HAD 2ND ACCIDENT OVER WEEKEND
HUSBAND has BROKEN RIBS IN HOSPITAL
HIT BY DRUNK RUNNING RED LIGHT
SURGERY TODAY

SIGNED JC.

Phoned ☐ Call Back ☒ Returned Call ☐ Wants To See You ☐ Will Call Again ☐ Was In ☐ See Operator ☐

1/2/76   10:45 AM   NO ANSWER
1/2/76   11:00 AM   BUSY
1/2/76   11:25 AM   BUSY
1/2/76   11:35 AM - Operator says line out of order.

1/2/76   11:45 AM   Spd LM & client that she should
call us because we can't reach her.

Put message form in client file when call is returned.

Can You Get Clients From Organizations?

Can you get clients from social, civic or charitable organizations? The answer to the question is simultaneously "Yes" and "No." If you join an organization solely to get clients, you will be wasting your time and money. The other members will see through you, and you won't get anything from them.

On the other hand, if you belong to an organization because you sincerely believe in its purposes and you work hard for the organization, the other members will be impressed by your efforts and how sincere and dedicated you are, and they will come to you with their legal work.

If you are going to pick an organization to work for with the hope of getting legal work, stay away from organizations which are heavily constituted of lawyers. It should be obvious that if 65% of the members of an organization are lawyers, there won't be as much legal work as there would be if you were the only lawyer. Some charities are so heavy with lawyers that they have a "Lawyers Division."

Some lawyers claim that you can get business simply by belonging to clubs and occasionally attending a meeting and making some noise so people know who you are. I think this was true years ago when very few people knew even one lawyer and would go to the lawyer they knew. The number of lawyers has more than doubled in the last 20 years and most people now can choose from many lawyers. Perhaps in some lower socio-economic organizations you can get business from the members simply by being the only lawyer and making some occasional noise, but it will be difficult.

The advice, "Above all, to thine own self be true" applies in this area.

Insurance Claims Adjusters: A Source of Clients

Insurance claims adjusters can be a very profitable source of clients in the personal injury and casualty fields. Insurance adjusters frequently are asked by their insureds to recommend an attorney to represent them against the other parties. Sometimes the adjuster will recommend an attorney, and sometimes not.

You must be very careful in your dealings with, and relations with, insurance adjusters.

Honest insurance adjusters will recommend an accident case to you if they think you are sincere, hard-working and competent, and if they like you. Adjusters will not ask for, or expect, any remuneration for recommending a client. Stay away from dishonest adjusters. Remember, all the dishonest adjuster has to lose is a job. You have a license to practice law to lose.

The best way to meet insurance adjusters is in connection with the cases you already have. When an adjuster makes first contact with you on a case, ask him or her to join you for lunch. You owe it to your client to meet the adjuster. Impress upon the adjuster that you are ready, willing and able to fight for your client to get your client what can reasonably be expected. Remember that impressions of you and your office may end up in the case file and may affect the amount of the settlement you can obtain for your client.

If the adjuster is impressed by you, you will obtain a better settlement for your client, and new cases may be referred to you. Remember that the recommendations of an insurance adjuster carry a lot of weight with accident victims. Work as hard and rapidly as you can on the referred matter. Remember that the first matter the adjuster refers to you may be a "real dog," as he or she may be testing you.

A lawyer can build a very profitable law practice on the referrals and recommendations of a single insurance adjuster. Just be very careful not to trespass the ethical prohibitions against soliciting.

How to Accept
Personal Injury Cases

I have written a special chapter on accepting personal injury cases because all lawyers, and especially new lawyers, run the risk of being called "Ambulance Chasers" if they act too quickly and "Negligent" if they act too slowly.

To begin with, the lawyer, when talking to the prospective client or family of the prospective client, should give the following advice (an exception to my warning about giving advice to people who are not yet your clients):

1. Engage a lawyer (whether it be you or somebody else) as rapidly as possible.

2. Do not discuss fault or facts with anybody except police officers until *after* they've consulted with a lawyer. (Usually there is a police report long before any lawyer is contacted.) If there is any possibility of criminal liability, then tell them not to talk to police officers either.

The client or potential client must be made to understand that it is essential for your investigator to photograph vehicle damage *before* the damage gets repaired. The adverse parties' statement must be gotten *before* they are instructed not to give statements. Third-party witnesses must be interviewed while their memory is fresh and before they move away. The scene of the accident must be examined and photographed *before* it is altered. Torn and blood-stained garments must *not* be thrown away at the hospital. Bruised and broken bodies should be photographed *before* healing.

The client or potential client must be made to understand that insurance companies have millions of dollars available for investigators and it is reasonable to assume that the insurance company will be into the case as soon as the other party reports the case to his or her insurance agent.

Criminal suspects get a Miranda warning advising them of availability of counsel. Personal injury victims don't get any such advice. If anything, over-zealous insurance adjustors sometimes tell the injured party *not* to get a lawyer, misrepresenting that the injured party will get a good recovery without the lawyer and that the lawyer is taking money which would otherwise go to the injured party.

The injured person must be made to understand that the insurance company's primary concern is to *defend* a claim for damages rather than getting any funds for their insured for personal injury. The injured party must also be made to understand that a personal injury claim must be valued and that the injured party doesn't have enough experience or knowledge to value it properly.

How to Protect Yourself

1. *Don't quote numbers or promise recoveries.* Tell the client orally and again in writing, "Based on the facts as they appear at the present time, it appears that you have a meritorious case. It is impossible to value the case until the full extent of injury, treatment, damages, and losses are known." Tell the client orally that anybody who promises or guarantees any specific recovery without knowing the extent of injury, etc., is either foolish or stupid or fraudulent.

2. *Get the client to sign more than one document.* We ask the client to sign and date the fee agreement and also to sign and date four "Authorities to Release Information." A client might say he didn't know what he was doing if he signed only one document, but he is hard pressed to make this claim when he has signed five times in five different places and dates his signatures five times in five different places.

3. *Try not to be present when the client actually signs and dates the fee agreement and authorities.* Have the client sign them out of your presence and either mail them back to you or have a friend or relative bring them back to you. If possible, have a friend or relative be with the injured party when the documents are signed. That friend or relative can later testify to your absence during the signing.

If necessary, leave the room yourself. Tell the injured party that you're going down the hall to the bathroom so that he or she can think about which lawyer to use without your presence. Knock on the door when you come back even if it's your own office you've left and come back to. Give the prospective client every reasonable opportunity not to use you.

4. *Begin work on the case immediately.* This is necessary not only to protect the client's own best interests, but also to substantiate the need for immediate legal help. If you told a client he or she needed a lawyer immediately and then did nothing for two weeks, you were either unethical for pressuring the client to sign or you were negligent in the conduct of the case, or both.

Re: Accident of _____(date)_____

Dear Mr. (or Ms.) Client:

This letter will confirm the details of our telephone discussion (our discussion in my office) on _____(date)_____ .

Our firm will represent you in your claim for damages as a result of the above accident. Our fee will be one-third (1/3) of any amounts obtained by settlement if a lawsuit is not necessary or forty per cent (40%) of all amounts received by settlement or judgment if filing of a lawsuit is necessary. If there is no recovery for you, there will be no fee.

We are enclosing herewith several authorities to obtain information. Please sign each where indicated by the red "X" as we need the authorities to obtain police reports, medical reports, etc. Additionally, please sign the enclosed copy of this letter and return the copy along with the authorities in the enclosed envelope. We cannot begin work until we have received back the copy of this letter and the authorities.

Very truly yours,

FOONBERG, CHAYO & GARDNER

By JAY G. FOONBERG

JGF:ak

(On Copies Only)
THE ABOVE IS UNDERSTOOD AND AGREED TO.

_____   _____
Signature   Date

Short Form Letter to Accept a PI Case

AUTHORITY TO RELEASE RECORDS

TO WHOM IT MAY CONCERN:

This is authority for you to furnish to my attorneys, FOONBERG, CHAYO & GARDNER or their representatives, all medical, police and financial reports pertaining to my accident which occurred on or about _____, 19____ at or about _____, _____, Calif.
      Street   City

_____   _____
    Dated   Signed

(Signed by _____ because victim is minor/
       (Relationship)
physically unable)

_____
   D.R. No.

Four copies of "Authority" form should be sent with fee letter.

How to Communicate
Settlement Offers
to Clients

Be sure that the client understands the difference between the *gross settlement* and the *net settlement* after costs, unpaid medical bills, and your fees. Send the client a letter explaining the breakdown and the *net* settlement. Clients are concerned about what *they* get, not about the gross settlement. When the insurance company sends a draft, get the client into the office to sign it. If you have to mail it to the client for signature, be sure to tell the client that it's a draft, not a check, and cannot be honored until *after* the insurance company compares your signature on the draft to your signature in their files. If you're stupid enough to endorse the draft before the client does, then you deserve to be deprived of your fee. Be careful about unpaid medical bills which have to be paid.

Failure to observe these rules is a very good way to get a complaint filed against you with the bar association.

Ms. (or Mr.) Client

    Re:

Dear Ms. Client:

    This letter will confirm our previous telephone conversation of _____. We have an offer from (insurance carrier) in the gross amount of _____.

    The gross settlement would be disbursed as follows:

Gross Amount			$
Less: Property Damage	$		
Out-of-Pocket Costs			
Police Report			
Medical Reports			
Filing Fee			
Service			
Total	$ _____		
		Balance	$ _____
Our Fee (as agreed)	$ _____		
		Balance	$ _____
Liens			$ _____
Dr.	$		$ _____
Net to You			$ _____

(Opt.) Please understand that the doctor bills are your responsibility and must be paid by you.

(Opt.) As we related to you by telephone, it is our opinion that your case has substantially more value. However, you would not realize this value for a significant length of time and we shall comply with your wishes to settle the case now. The case is your case and we undertook to prosecute it fully and had you wished, we would have rejected the offer and tried the case to judgment although this would have caused a substantial delay in your obtaining funds.

(Opt.) If the above is acceptable and agreeable to you, please sign and date the enclosed copy of this letter and return to me in the envelope provided.
(On Copies Only)—THE ABOVE IS UNDERSTOOD AND AGREEABLE TO ME.

Date: _____   Signed: _____

Can You Get Clients
by Running for
Political Office?

I really can't answer this question for you. The answer will depend on your area. I've listed this question solely to call the possibility to your attention.

Running for office will give you exposure. You will address many groups and may get radio, TV or newspaper coverage. You will get good insights into what people feel are the significant issues in your community. People who see and hear you or read about you will learn your views. Some of these people may identify with you and wish to use you as a lawyer.

On the other hand, if you run and lose, people may avoid you and want to go to the winner. The time, energy and money you invest in an unsuccessful political campaign may have been much better spent in your practice.

If you are thinking of running for political office with the plan or hope of increasing your practice through publicity whether you win or lose, I would suggest some homework on your part before you start.

Contact some of the lawyers in your community who ran for office and lost during the last few years. Ask them if, on balance, the campaign exposure enhanced or damaged the development of their law practice. Ask them if they would do it again.

Based on my very limited questioning, I believe that running for political office and losing might help you in rural areas but might be disastrous in an urban area.

Getting Paid Work from Lawyer Reference Services

List yourself with every lawyer reference service that will accept your listing. The listing fees are nominal (usually $5.00 to $25.00 per year), in addition to the cost of the bar association dues, and the lawyer reference service will refer you many matters over the years.

Lawyer reference services are allowed to advertise to the laity in phone books and in other places. People new to a community often turn to such lawyer reference services for help in selecting a lawyer.

Not too many years ago, people went to a bar association for referral because they simply didn't know any lawyers. Today, I suspect people go to bar associations for referrals because they know too many lawyers and don't know how to select one. They believe that the lawyers who list themselves as being available through the bar association are likely to be the better lawyers, or they believe (sometimes erroneously, sometimes correctly) that the bar association lawyer referral service will refer them to a lawyer most likely to be able to help them. The public is aware of the fact that all lawyers specialize to some degree and that not all lawyers are willing or competent to handle all cases.

There is no way of knowing or guessing whether you'll get your first significant matter in weeks, months, or years. However, sooner or later you will get a significant matter, and the investment will be repaid handsomely. Additionally, you are helping the public by making lawyers (including yourself) available.

I recommend that you make the financial investment in the lawyer reference services.

Getting Legal Fees and Work
from the Government

With the recent huge increase in the number of new lawyers, this kind of work is becoming increasingly difficult to obtain. How much of this work is available and how well or poorly it is compensated depends upon your local situation.

All I can do is to give you some typical examples and typical sources and you'll have to get the information yourself.

Types of Work

1. *Conflict of Interests.* It is common where there are multiple defendants that a single lawyer or department cannot represent some of them, and either the court or the government agency appoints and pays for the representation of the others.

2. *Juveniles.* It is common for a probate or juvenile court to appoint a lawyer to represent the interests of a child or unborn child.

3. *Appeals.* Commonly, because of indigency or conflict of interests, a lawyer can be appointed for the appeal even though another lawyer or government agency represented the appellant or respondent at trial.

4. *Indigents.* Indigents generally are entitled to free representation (meaning someone else is paying), both in civil and criminal matters. There are various agencies which pay for private lawyers for indigents.

Sources of Work

Getting this type of work may be very easy or very difficult, depending on how profitable (or unprofitable) it is and depending upon the method of lawyer selection.

1. Judges (federal, state and local) are the most common sources of appointments. Sometimes each judge has his or her own list or own system of choosing lawyers and sometimes judges are obligated to use a master "approved" list. Ask the judge's clerk how the judge picks or selects a lawyer when a court-appointed lawyer is necessary. If the judge makes the selection, make an appointment to see the judge to tell him or her you are available. If there are too many judges, ask around to see which judges or departments make the largest number of appointments. See those judges and mail a résumé to the other judges. Tell the other judges that you are a new lawyer available for appointments. Ask them to keep the letter for several months even if there is no immediate need for you.

2. Public defender and legal aid (federal, state and local) attorneys. Contact responsible people in the offices to find out how outside lawyers are selected in conflict cases and how you can get on the list.

3. Contact appeals court clerks (state and federal) to find out about getting appointed for indigent appeals.

4. Contact various state, federal and local administrative agencies which seek private practice attorneys. Naturally, you won't know which ones do until you ask. In some jurisdictions, this conduct may not be permissible. Therefore, you will have to ask how to ask the agencies ethically.

Be Persistent

Getting some of this work may be difficult. Sometimes clerks will tell you that the judges have no time to see you. This may be true, but possibly the clerk has some favorites and wants to keep you off the list. These government appointments might be someone's private political slush fund. You may step on a few toes, but you may also end up with some cash fees and experience right away.

Getting Legal Work and Fees
from Other Lawyers

Can you get legal work from other lawyers? You not only *can* get legal work from other lawyers, I recommend that you *should* seek work from them.

Solicitation of work from another *lawyer* is perfectly proper. Solicitation from the laity is improper. Ethical consideration EC 2-22 allows a lawyer to associate with a lawyer outside of his or her firm with the consent of the client.

DR 2-103's *only prohibition* is recommending yourself for employment to *nonlawyers*. There is no prohibition against recommending yourself to *lawyers*.

Many lawyers, especially sole practitioners, have low-fee legal work that they don't want to handle, or can't economically devote the time to. Additionally, overburdened and underpaid lawyers, particularly sole practitioners, are an excellent source of immediate legal fees and immediate work for the new lawyer. The problem is one of making your availability known to sole practitioners. They frequently are so busy that they have no time to see you even though they need your help as badly as you need income.

Most sole practitioners dislike leaving their office for minor matters. Most have a backlog and an ongoing flow of relatively low-pay, low-profit matters which they are only too happy to refer out to you if they know you exist.

The following kinds of cases can be obtained from overburdened lawyers:

1. Low-pay domestic relations matters. There are many people who just don't qualify for legal aid or other public lawyers but who need legal services and can pay a little. Five hundred dollars may be a reason-

able fee for a default divorce, but the client may only be able to pay $175.00 or $200.00. The established practitioner with established overhead can't economically handle this case. You can, because you don't have the overhead yet. It's a quick fee and some legal experience for you.

2. Landlord-tenant disputes. No lawyer or client enjoys this kind of work, representing either the landlords or the tenants. Here again you can handle an eviction proceeding for a relatively low fee due to your lack of overhead and need for experience, and at the same time relieve another lawyer of an unwanted matter.

3. Out-of-office minor court appearances and minor proceedings. Lawyers don't like leaving their office for a whole morning for some simple matter that will take a short time. Typical examples are: perfunctory court appearances for such matters as continuances or minor judgment/debtor examinations. Attendance at depositions (where the deposition is a great distance from the office) and attendance at medical examinations are other examples.

In short, you do both yourself and the sole practitioner a favor when you handle a relatively minor matter at $15.00 an hour plus $0.25 a mile. The $45.00 you are paid for the morning will enable a solo to earn $200.00 or more in the office.

4. Research, pleadings, investigations. These areas are covered by professional organizations and, unless you are in a geographic area where they don't yet exist, you shouldn't try to sell yourself to other lawyers on this basis. Once you "get your foot in the door" with the sole practitioner, you will get work of this nature, but you are competing with nonlawyers such as law students, etc., who actively solicit this business.

5. Minor low-pay criminal and traffic court matters. Here again there are people who want to contest a speeding ticket but who can't pay more than $100.00 or $200.00. The established practitioner can't handle the matter at this price, but you can and should, both to fulfill the clients' need for legal services and to earn some money as well as get experience. To obtain this work, you have to make the other lawyer aware of your existence and availability to do this kind of work. The easiest way is to locate yourself as close to as many sole practitioners as possible. Locate yourself in a suite of sole practitioner lawyers or in a building with sole practitioners or in a block or in a neighborhood or town with as many sole practitioners as possible, as close as possible. Introduce yourself to each of them. Sit next to them at the bar

association meetings. Tell them plainly and simply of your availability to do the kind of legal work described above.

Don't steal clients. Remember, you are being selected by the lawyer, not by the client. You want more work from the lawyer who is paying you. Therefore, when the "client" asks you to handle another matter, you are obligated to refer the client back to the referring lawyer.

Remember, the overburdened sole practitioner wants to give you the work to get it off his or her desk. You must be aggressive and make yourself known to these lawyers as being available. Get close to them physically by being in the same suite, building, block or area. Take them to lunch. Walk in on them and announce yourself. You have nothing to lose.

At least one state bar is attempting to match the new lawyers' need for fees with the overburdened sole practioner's need for help in a statewide service with a view toward giving the low-fee private practice client good service. In my opinion, this "matching" process may be the greatest impetus to private practice growth since casualty insurance.

Minority Work
and Money

Minority Work

In this section I only wish to suggest a concept. The particular fact situation is so complex that all I can do is make some general suggestions and give you a few examples and then it's up to you to start making telephone calls and writing letters. The availability or non-availability of what I call minority work changes according to your particular locality and the politics of your particular minority or location.

What I call "minority money" is also called "set-aside" money or "affirmative-action" money or by other names. Many agencies' rules require private companies and semi-public entities such as public utilities and investment firms to set aside funds to use minority firms.

Many federal and state appropriation bills contain clauses that a certain percentage of the work must be awarded to minority-owned or operated businesses depending on the particular person administering the particular program at the particular time. This may or may not vary to include awarding contracts to minority law firms to do some of the legal work. Sometimes this minority legal work is awarded as a matter of policy rather than a matter of law, so you'll have to dig around until you find the person in the government agency or the company who is responsible for "affirmative action" programs. You may find that the company or agency has a well-defined policy or program that includes attorneys or you may have to convince them that you should be the first attorney firm hired under a new program which you will help design.

Minority Money

Again depending upon the time, the place, and the facts, there may be minority money available to you if you can qualify.

Often banks as a matter of company policy or the Small Business Administration or other agencies may loan or guarantee loans to minority businesses. I have heard of white lawyers going into partnerships with black lawyers or Spanish-surname lawyers to get access to the money for starting a law practice.

If you are a minority lawyer, or know a minority lawyer, you should consider this avenue of financing. Unfortunately, you'll have to do the leg work to get more information.

How to Get More Legal Work from Existing Clients

A satisfied client will produce more clients and generate more business for you than any other single source. There are two ways in which existing clients can generate business:

1. *They can bring in new clients.* A satisfied client is your most likely and probable source of new clients. Clients who have been well served have all of the zeal of missionaries. They can't wait to brag to friends and relatives and co-workers about what a great lawyer they have. They will recommend many clients to you over the years.

2. *They can bring you their own repeat business.* As a general rule, clients want more attention, not less attention from their lawyer. They are willing to pay for legal work if only the attorney is available to do it.

The attorney who shows a genuine interest in the welfare of a client will find that the client will want the lawyer to do "whatever is necessary" to keep the client's legal matters in order. The attorney who stays in close touch with clients will get a telephone call from the client ("Before I sign this lease, I want you to look at it"), which will not happen if the attorney is inaccessible to the client.

After 10 years in practice, I set up a 20-year follow-up calendar. I wish I had started my first day. The following are examples of "follow-up" legal work, often required by clients, and commonly neglected by lawyers:

A. *Corporate Minutes.* Most corporations have periodic meetings of their governing bodies, at least annually, if not more often. You should send a reminder letter about 30 days prior to meetings. There is nothing unethical in reminding the client of the meetings requirement. In most instances, the client will ask you for help in setting the agenda and preparing the minutes. The client will be happy to pay you and will be grateful to you for the reminder. In some instances, the client will ignore your letter. In my opinion, anything more than one letter starts bordering on solicitation.

B. *Lease Options.* Whether your client is the owner or the tenant, the lease may have options for renewal or for purchase. A letter to the client about 90 days before the option date will often lead to your doing legal work for the client.

C. *Wills.* A letter should be sent to the client about five years after the will is drafted, reminding the client that five years have elapsed, and that a will review would be appropriate.

D. *Judgment Renewals.* A letter should be sent about a year before a judgment becomes unenforceable.

E. *Minors Becoming Adults.* Minors often are entitled to receive funds upon attaining majority. The funds may be from previous settlements, inheritances, trust terminations, etc.

F. *Annual Statements of Officers for Corporations.* In most states, an annual statement of officers of a corporation must be filed with the Secretary of State, and a letter reminding the client of the deadline is appropriate. In some cases, the form may be sent directly to you, if you have formed the corporation for the client, in which case you will send the form to the client for signature, with a short note of explanation.

G. *Fictitious Name Statement.* A periodic letter to your business or corporate clients reminding them to file fictitious name statements for their various entities is often in order. Additionally, reminding clients that businesses which are not longer doing business should file an Abandonment of Fictitious Name could be an important reminder for the client, and additional legal work for you.

H. *Expungement of Prior Criminal Records.*

The above list is not intended to be exclusive. Depending upon your local practice situation, and your desire to be of service to your clients, there are many more possibilities.

The important things to remember are:

1. When you finish a particular assignment for a client, close the file, and calendar future work which the client may need. (See Closed File form in chapter on "Simple Filing Systems for the New Lawyer.")

2. Remember that the client welcomes your reminders.

3. Don't send more than one reminder (thus avoiding the problem of solicitation).

4. Don't worry that your reminders may generate work for another lawyer; you'll get your share.

How to Recognize and Handle Conflicts of Interest

Any time you are representing more than one person in a matter, ask yourself if there is a conflict of interest. Remember that corporations and partnerships are "persons" for purposes of conflicts of interest. If there appears to be a conflict, explain the potential conflict to the client *in writing* and get permission *in writing* to continue the representation. If you can't do this, pick one client at the beginning and tell the other to get another lawyer.

New lawyers are especially prone to problems involving conflicts of interests for the following reasons:

1. They don't recognize the problem when they see it.

2. They don't know how to handle the problem when they recognize it.

3. They are afraid to broach this subject for fear of frightening the client away and losing a fee.

4. They don't realize they can still do the work and gain a fee if the conflict problem is properly handled.

The importance of recognizing and solving conflicts of interests at the beginning has two aspects:

To you as the lawyer: If you don't recognize and solve the problem:

1. You may have to withdraw from the case.

2. You may not be able to collect any fees due you.

3. You may have to refund any fees previously paid you.

4. Depending on the extent of the problem, you may be disciplined or disbarred for your stupidity.

To the client: The client will have to obtain a new lawyer and waste a lot of time and energy locating and educating the new lawyer. This delay might even prejudice the case.

How to recognize a conflict of interest problem:

Simple Conflicts. These are conflicts between you and the client. To the extent that lawyers are compensated by clients and clients compensate them, there is always a theoretical conflict between the client and the lawyer. This theoretical conflict comes close to being actual when the lawyer is compensated by "a piece of the action." This problem, however, is normally treated by bar associations under the category of "unreasonable" or "excessive" fees rather than conflict of interests.

These simple conflicts also can arise when you have two clients unrelated to each other such as:

1. Client A wants you to collect $1,000.00 from X and Client B wants to collect $3,000.00 from the same X. X only has or is even likely to have $500.00. Who would get it? Client A or Client B or both A and B in some ratio?

2. Client A wants you to argue as a lawyer for a debtor that involuntary repossessions are unconstitutional and Client B wants you to argue to the same or a different court in a different matter than involuntary repossessions are constitutional. Do you take both cases on the theory that the court makes the law and not the lawyer?

Complex Conflicts. These are the more common situations and arise out of the fact that multiple parties want to use only one lawyer, typically to save fees. The most common situations are:

1. *Partnerships.* Each partner and the partnership are independent entities and there are conflicts and potential conflicts in the situation.

2. *Corporations.* Each incorporator, each director, each officer, each employee, and the corporation are independent and could have conflicting interests.

3. *Divorce.* Usually the husband and wife have conflicting interests in a divorce. In theory, the court represents the children. In some jurisdictions another lawyer is appointed to represent the children.

4. *Multiple defendants or potential defendants in criminal cases.* The defendants may later wish to turn on each other or try to get immunity in exchange for testimony.

5. *Auto Accident Cases.* (a) Insufficient insurance or assets. There may not be sufficient insurance or assets to cover all of the injured parties. For example, suppose the defendant has a $15,000-$30,000 policy and there are four parties seriously injured in your client's car. Suppose that the claims of each are reasonably worth $20,000 or more.

Suppose further that the defendant is an indigent who can successfully go bankrupt on personal injury judgment debts. Suppose further that the insurance company is willing to pay in the entire $30,000. If you take all four cases, how do you divide up the insurance money? Can you take all four cases? Which client(s) do you keep or reject? If you advise one or more people to get independent counsel (probably the lesser value cases), should you explain why? Would an explanation be a conflict with the clients you keep?

(b) Passenger or driver. Can you represent both the driver and the passengers? Is there a possibility of suing the driver/owner for negligent operation or maintenance of the vehicle, or under a guest statue?

6. *Other Conflict-Of-Interest Situations.* Obviously, there is an infinite number of possible conflict-of-interest situations. Any time you have or may have more than one client in a matter you should ask yourself, "Do I have a conflict-of-interest situation here?" If you are not sure, call another lawyer for an opinion or call the local bar association and get the name of a member of the ethics committee. (Some ethics committess will only answer requests of the bar association itself, however, as opposed to individual members of the bar association. And some ethics committee members will only respond to written questions for fear of misunderstanding of the facts.)

You should get another lawyer's opinion of the situation to protect both yourself and the client. The opinion of an older, more experienced lawyer can help you decide whether or not you have a conflict, and the fact that you were concerned over the possibility of a conflict and took steps to get another opinion or other opinions would probably be of help to you in the event of a subsequent problem.

How to handle the problem:

Be honest, be forthright, and put everything in writing!

The Code of Professional Responsibility does *not* prohibit your representing clients when there is or might be a conflict of interests. The lawyer may represent more than one party provided the client understands the conflict and waives it. Below is a form letter for conflict-of-interest problems (I use the same or similar language in my oral discussions in the office):

Name and address of Client

Re: (Matter involved)

Dear _____:

I am writing to you to repeat in writing what I told
you earlier in the office. I cannot commence work on your
case until you have returned the enclosed copy of this letter indicating your preference.

As I explained to you in the office, a lawyer cannot
be on both sides of a fence; nor can a lawyer ethically
represent people who may have conflicting interests
unless they understand they may have conflicting interests and still wish to use the same lawyer to do the
work by waiving the conflicts.

Partnerships, Corporations, Business Ventures

Each of you is a legal entity and in the eyes of the
law, the partnership is a legal entity. Theoretically, each
of the three of you should have a different lawyer to protect your respective interests.

I can draft your partnership agreement to conform
to what you have agreed to and can raise additional problems which have to be solved by you, but I cannot take
sides.

Alternative 1:

In the event of a dispute between you I shall have
the right to withdraw from the case and not take either
side.

Alternative 2:

In the event of a dispute between "A" and you, you
must understand that I would have to represent "A" since
"A" is actually my client.

Alternative 3:

In the event of a dispute between you, you have agreed that my client will be the partnership and you understand that I would not represent either of you personally.

Alternative 4:

In the event of a dispute between you, I will choose a client between you.

I would not intentionally favor one of you over the other but you may feel more comfortable with a lawyer who is actively representing your individual personal interest.

Divorces

You asked me to represent both of you in order to save legal fees and costs.

You told me how you wanted the assets and liabilities handled and the amounts you have agreed on for alimony and child support. I explained to you that if you wished to fight in court, a judge might give either of you more or less assets or more or less alimony. I explained that the issue of child support cannot be bargained solely between you and that the court keeps jurisdiction to decide child support and custody regardless of what you have agreed to. I have also cautioned you on the necessity of making full disclosure of all assets, liabilities, income, expenses, etc., and that the intentional or negligent omission of important facts might cause a court to overturn the whole agreement in future years.

I also explained to you that in later years it may be relevant who was the plaintiff and who was the defendant in the divorce action and that it was possible for each of you to sue the other for divorce.

You indicated that notwithstanding your rights, you wished to proceed with the divorce as a default proceeding and to make the provisions you have agreed upon.

Multiple Defendants

In a Criminal Proceeding

You have indicated that you wish to be represented together and I indicated to you that you are each entitled to individual, separate counsel and that if you can't pay for separate counsel, a public defender may be available. I also informed you that you may wish to "finger point" at each other or that one of you may be able to receive immunity from prosecution for testifying against the other.

In Auto Accident Cases

I explained to you that there may not be enough insurance or assets for all of you to recover what you are entitled to and you indicated that if this should happen you would divide the total proceeds between yourselves as you will agree and that if you can't agree, the funds will be held in my trust account while you arbitrate between yourselves the share that each of you is entitled to. I would not represent either of you in any such arbitration, which would be at additional expense to each of you.

How to Keep Clients

What do clients want from you? There is often a difference between what people want and will pay for as opposed to what they need.

Often a person will happily pay for what is *wanted,* but resents paying for what is *needed,* if the two differ. Think of your own situation when you are sick. You'd pay anything within reason for a physician to make a house call. It is much more efficient and economical for you to go to the physician's office, but you'd still prefer a house call. You need a $35 office visit, but you want and would pay for a $100 house call. The supply-and-demand situation between new physicians and patients is such that new physicians can turn down business they used to welcome. Unfortunately for you, the supply-and-demand situation between new lawyers and the need for legal services is in a different balance, and you must give clients what they want.

The purpose of the comparison is solely to emphasize the difference between providing a client what is *wanted* and providing what is *needed* (these are not mutually exclusive).

Therefore, the gist of this chapter is to teach you the things that clients *want* in *addition* to your efforts and in *addition* to good results.

1. *Effort vs. Results.* New lawyers think that clients want results more than they want effort. Believe it or not, the reverse is true. Clients *need* favorable results; they *want* effort. Don't misinterpret what I am saying. I am *not* saying that clients don't care whether they win or lose. They care very much. I am saying that whether they come back to you when a matter is over with, or whether they recommend other clients to you or pay your fee willingly, or not at all, is determined more by their opinion of your efforts than their opinion of the results.

2. *How to Project Efforts.* Listed below are things you can do to let

the client know you are putting forth effort. It is *not true* that the practice of law is like the proverbial iceberg, with 90% hidden. It *is true* that there are lazy lawyers and lawyers who really don't care about their clients, and who obscure under a basket 90% of what they are doing.

A. Send your client a copy of EVERY document you produce, including correspondence, pleadings, briefs, etc., as you produce it.

B. Send your client a copy of all incoming documents as they are received, including pleadings, correspondence, etc.

C. Return your client's calls immediately, or have someone else return them. Remember this:

    1. I needed a lawyer;

    2. I couldn't get in touch with you;

    3. I got another lawyer;

    4. I don't need you any more . . .

D. If you work on your client's case in the evening or on a weekend, call him or her at home to ask some questions, so that he or she knows you are devoting your "personal" time to the matter.

E. Bill monthly.

F. Make "house calls."

G. One of the most effective techniques I employ is to visit clients at their places of business.

    1. Visit your client's place of business to understand that business. Don't charge for the time you spend going through the factory, but do charge for the conference at the place of business to the same extent as you would have charged for the same conference in your office.

    2. Go with your client to the scene of the accident in personal injury and worker's compensation cases. This will really impress your client as to your effort.

    3. Go to the medical examination with your client when the defense doctor makes an examination.

H. Inform clients of new cases or statutes which come to your attention that affect their affairs. They will appreciate your concern. They will feel you care about them and are putting forth effort for them.

How to Lose Clients

Why Do Clients Leave?

According to a national survey,

1% die

3% move

5% dislike the product

24% have some dispute which does not get adjusted

67% leave because they feel they were treated discourteously, indifferently, or simply were not given good service.

Cases and Clients that Should Be Turned Down

Abraham Lincoln reputedly advised a new lawyer on passing the bar, "Young man, it's more important to know what cases not to take than it is to know the law."

As a new lawyer with relatively little case load, you'll want to take almost any case from almost any client. The more experienced lawyer knows better. It is most crucial that you recognize that you need cash, as well as satisfaction in helping the downtrodden, if you intend to be in practice the second or third year. Therefore, I am going to list cases and clients that you should turn down during your first year or two. After you're established and can afford the luxury of laying out your time and money to be a "swell person," or to gamble on profitability, then you might wish to take these cases.

This list is based upon my personal experiences and you may wish to expand or contract it as time goes by.

When You Are the Second or Third Lawyer on the Case

Be very careful. There may be honest personality differences between the client and prior lawyers but multiple lawyers often indicate:

A nonmeritorious case;

An uncooperative client;

A nonpaying client.

Check with the prior lawyers before accepting the case. Ask the prior lawyers if there is an unpaid bill involved. If, after checking, you believe in the client and the merits of prosecution, then by all means accept the case if you want to.

If you do take the case, you should — whenever possible — communicate with the adverse lawyer or party to make clear the reasons for multiple lawyers, if you can do so without violating attorney-client privilege and without further damaging the case. The other side may, and probably will, equate multiple lawyers with the three problems stated, and your coming in as lawyer number three may harm your client's case and your economics. If you can't explain the multiple lawyer problem to the other side, then keep in mind that you'll have a more difficult and perhaps impossible task reaching a fair settlement without a trial to judgment.

"Hurt Feeling" Cases

This type of case usually has wrongful conduct by the defendant, but no provable special damages on the part of your client, or nominal damages at best. The case and your compensation are dependent on either presumed or punitive damages. Examples of this type of case are:

A. Libel and slander
B. Bar room brawls
C. Most assault and battery cases

Landlord-Tenant Cases (Unless You Are Paid in Full in Advance)

It makes no difference if you represent the landlord or the tenant, your client will never be happy and will never pay you *after* the case is over. Landlords greatly resent having to pay you money to evict someone who is already delinquent in rent or who is busting up the place, or driving other tenants away with such activities as drag racing in the driveway at 4 a.m., or having all night pot and bongo parties. Tenants often want to leave but want to blackmail the landlord into paying them something to leave. Sometimes tenants can't leave because they haven't got the first and last month's rent to move into another place. Sometimes tenants feel they are being unreasonably evicted because they made what to them is a reasonable request which the landlord ignored, such as fixing the leaky, noisy toilet.

Landlord-tenant disputes are often more vindicitve than divorce suits, and each side wants to use the lawyer for revenge if they can use the lawyer for free.

Divorce Cases for People Heavily in Debt (Unless You Are Paid in Advance)

Please remember that poor people can get divorces through legal aid. In most—if not almost all—cases, divorce is an economic diaster for everyone involved. There is rarely enough money to support the parties and children living apart. I am not a qualified expert on the subject of causes of divorce cases, but I believe that economic insecurity is a major factor in divorce. In accepting or not accepting divorce cases it is safe to assume that the retainer money up front may be the only money you'll see. Be firm in getting the money up front. Court orders awarding you a fee of one-half of the fair amount at the rate of $15.00 a month if the breadwinner sticks around aren't worth much. Don't blame the court. Blame yourself for accepting a case legal aid would have taken.

Criminal Cases (Unless You Get Paid in Advance)

A person in prison doesn't earn much more than cigarette money. Don't take clients that should be represented by the public defender.

Slip Falls (Unless There Are Substantial Damages)

Even the most meritorious slip fall is hard to settle for a fair amount short of trial. You'll spend huge amounts of time and have very little to show for your efforts.

Bankruptcies (Unless You Are Paid in Advance in Full)

It was embarrassing when my client amended his bankruptcy schedules to include the unpaid balance of the fee due me.

Clients Who Loudly Proclaim That You Can Have All the Money Recovered; They Are "Only Interested in the Principle"

These cases fall into the same category as the "Hurt Feeling" cases.

Clients Who Want to Use Your Telephones, Secretary, and Offices to Do Their Business

I don't know why, but this type of client always seems to end up "trouble." Be forewarned.

Clients Who Ask for a Loan of Money Against Their Case

You'd be surprised at how many new lawyers get stuck lending small amounts of money to clients. When clients say that if you don't lend them some money they'll have to go to another lawyer who will lend them money, then you're better off without those clients.

Cases Where "They'll Settle Right Away Because They Can't Afford the Publicity of Litigation"

When a prospective client makes this statement, I cringe. Usually the person honestly believes what is said. Unfortunately, it never happens this way. For some reason the adverse party in this type of case will consider discussing a possible settlement as soon as the United States Supreme Court denies *certiorari*. When you hear these magic words, convince the client that a noncontingency hourly rate payable in advance is best for him or her. Convince such a client that a contingency fee in such a case would overcompensate you as the lawyer in view of the early anticipated settlement of the case.

Cases Totally Without Merit

If a case has no chance, be honest; tell the client you won't handle a case totally without merit.

The next chapter will give you some techniques for saying "No" to the prospective client.

Keep in mind that you are not obligated to take cases that could and probably should be handled by publicly funded lawyers such as those in legal aid and publice defender offices. Remember also that if your fee agreement is properly drafted, you can withdraw from the case. But don't forget that you cannot hold onto the client and stop working due to an unpaid fee.

How to Say "No" to a Client or Case

For a new lawyer, cases and clients are hard to come by. You'll be afraid to say "No" when a case or client should be turned down. Lawyers by nature like to be "nice people." Lawyers also want as many clients as possible and don't like to get rid of clients or cases. The suggestions of this chapter may help you in a difficult situation.

Tell Your Client the Truth

Ninety-five percent of the problems will disappear when you tell your client the truth.

A. *No Merit to Case.* Tell your client that, in your opinion, the case is without merit. Tell the client that you'd like to take the case and make money but there just isn't a case.

B. *Uneconomical Case.* Tell the client that although he or she is legally in the right, the economics of the case just don't warrant the use of a lawyer.

Suggest Alternatives

A. *Small Claims Court.* Suggest in the smaller cases that the client use the services of the Small Claims Court and keep all the money without sharing it with lawyers.

B. *Other Lawyers.* Suggest that the client seek the opinion of another lawyer who might disagree with your evaluation.

C. Give the client the phone numbers of legal aid, public defender, bar association referral system, consumer advocate offices, etc., so that the client will know where to go for help.

D. Suggest that certain clients represent themselves. In some situations, such as landlord-tenant conflicts, you can teach landlord clients what they have to know to represent themselves. Let them know they are paying you for their education.

Put It in Writing

After you decline the case or client, send a follow-up letter confirming what you told the client, including the suggestion to contact another lawyer and repeating the phone numbers. This will be of great help to you in protecting yourself if the client denies the conversation.

Ask Your Client for "Money Up Front"

Asking clients to put their money where their mouths are will help get rid of unwanted clients who know a case is nonmeritorious.

Believe it or not, the honest, legitimate client wants the truth. The client won't be angry with you for hearing bad news. You'll be respected and that client will come back in the future.

Part V
Setting Fees

The Fee and Representation Letter

The importance of the fee-representation agreement cannot be over-emphasized. It will help eliminate disputes between you and your client more effectively than any other procedure.

The fee letter can best be explained by using an all-inclusive example and then exploring the importance of the various parts:

John Client
123 Main Street
Anytown, U.S.A.

(1)   RE: Jones vs. Smith; breach of contract

Dear Mr. Jones:

     This letter will confirm our office discussion
(2) of Thursday, January 4th.

     It was a pleasure meeting with you in our office. As I explained to you, it is my opinion that you defin-
(3) itely need the assistance of a lawyer, whether it be our
(4) firm or another lawyer. In my opinion, the matter is too complex for you to represent yourself.

(5)   As I explained to you, if you wish us to repre-
(6) (7) sent you, our fee will be $1,500.00 to prepare the complaint, do written interrogatories, take the deposition of Mr. Smith if necessary, and appear for the first day
(8) in court. If any additional work is required for such things as motions, additional depositions or additional
(9) days in court, you will be charged at our hourly rate of $95.00 per hour. If the case is settled short of trial, the
(10) fee will still be a minimum of $1,500.00.

(11)   The above does not include any out-of-pocket costs which may be incurred, such as court filing fees, sheriff's fees, deposition costs, photocopying, etc. We estimate, but cannot guarantee, that these costs will

(12)   run between $250.00 and $350.00, and, as explained, these costs are in addition to our fee and are <u>not</u> included in the $1,500.00 fee.

(13)   You indicated that you wished to pay in installments of $350.00 fees and $100.00 costs to begin work, and $150.00 fees and $50.00 costs the first of each month until you are current, and then, additional fees and costs will be paid monthly, as billed.

        This schedule is acceptable to us, so long as you understand that if you terminate payments, we may

(14)   terminate our services and withdraw from the case.

(15)   As I indicated to you, based on the facts as you related them to me in the office, you should win, and you should be awarded a judgment of between $9,500.00 and $15,000.00, unless the case is settled at a different sum. Obviously, depending upon the facts as they are developed, our opinion could change and you could be awarded more or less, or even lose. You

(16)   also understand that getting a judgment is not the same as getting cash and that you may have to expend additional costs and fees to collect the judgment.

(17)   You asked me if spending money on legal fees in this case is throwing good money after bad, and I told you that at this point, I couldn't give you an answer, and that you should understand that there are no guarantees of winning or collecting.

        It is my opinion, however, that whether you use our firm or other lawyers, you should proceed with

(18)   your case. Please do not delay. If you delay the commencement of your suit, you may at some point be barred from bringing it.

(19)   If the above properly sets forth our agreement, please sign and return the enclosed copy of this

(20)   letter, along with a check in the amount of $450.00, payable to my trust account. I will draw $350.00 toward my fees, and leave $100.00 toward costs as outlined above. A self-addressed, postage-paid envelope is enclosed for your convenience.

(21)
If we do not receive the signed copy of this letter, and your check, within 30 days, I shall assume that you have obtained other counsel, and shall mark my file "closed" and do nothing further.

(22)
If any of the above is not clear, or if you have any question, please do not hesitate to call.

Very truly yours

To be typed on the copy of the letter:

The above is understood and agreed to, and my check in the amount of $450.00, payable to Jane Attorney Trust Account is enclosed.

(23)
Dated: _____   _____

John Client

Essential Points to the Fee and Representation Letter

Obviously, the fee-representation letter must be tailor-made to the particular facts of the matter and the fee. Whatever form you decide to use, your letter should include the following:

(1) *The Matter Involved.* Perhaps your client has several legal matters, and has not told you about any of them except the Smith matter. This should prevent a later claim that you were responsible for *more* than this matter.

(2) *Your Interview Date.* This establishes when you had an interview to get the facts. This is for your protection in the event you are sued by your client or another party.

(3) *Whether or Not a Lawyer Is Required.* This avoids the interviewee claiming that you said no lawyer was necessary and that he or she should "forget about it."

(4) *Suggesting Other Lawyers.* Suggest the client may wish to see another lawyer. This relates to not representing the client until the agreement is returned. (See point 21 of this chapter.)

(5) *If You Wish Us to Represent You.* This reinforces that you are not yet the lawyer, and don't yet have responsibility.

(6) *The Amount of the Fee.* This establishes what I call the "Basic Fee."

(7) *Describing the Work the Fee Covers.* This discusses what you will do for the Basic Fee.

(8) *What the Basic Fee Does NOT Cover.* This describes what is not included in the Basic Fee.

(9) *Additional Work Fee Arrangement.* How you will charge for the work that is *not* included in this Basic Fee.

(10) *Minimum Fee.* What the minimum fee will be.

(11) *Out-of-Pocket Costs.* The client will not understand the difference between costs and fees, unless you explain it. This reinforces your explanation.

(12) *Addition to Fees.* Reinforce that out-of-pocket costs are in addition to fees.

(13) *Payment Schedule.* Set forth the cash flow that you have agreed upon, to avoid later misunderstandings.

(1) *Right to Terminate Services.* It is important that the client understands your right to terminate services for nonpayment. In some jurisdictions there may be ethical considerations in domestic relations and criminal matters. This portion should satisfy the requirements of DR 2-110(C)(1)(e) so that you can withdraw when the client stops paying.

(15) *Your Opinion of the Merits of the Case.* Repeat in a letter what you told the client in the office, and that what you said was based upon the facts which were given you. (Obviously, you may use this part of your letter to state that you are not yet in a position to express an opinion as to the outcome, or that you won't be able to express an opinion until research is done or until discovery is underway or completed.) In some types of work, you can quote dollar amounts. In some types, such as personal injury, you should not. Always repeat in writing what you did or did not say in the office to prevent later problems when the client claims you quoted a large recovery.

(16) *Explain Judgments.* Be sure the client is aware that winning a case and getting a judgment for fees and costs is not the same as getting cash, and that many judgments are uncollectible.

(17) *No Guarantees.* The client should understand that you have *not* guaranteed the outcome, and that it is possible that the funds expended on legal fees won't guarantee results.

(18) *Tell Client Not to Delay.* Warn the prospective client in lay language not to delay. Warn the prospective client that laches or a Statute of Limitations can prejudice the case if there are delays. *Do not* express an opinion on the statute date, unless you are engaged to do so. If you gave the client the wrong date, you could have malpractice liability.

(19) *Signing and Returning Copy of Letter.* Obviously, the signed copy in effect becomes a fee contract when returned to you.

(20) *Repeat* that both letter and check should be returned.

(21) *Set Date for Return of Engagement Letter.* Clearly indicate that you will assume the "client" has obtained other help to prevent the "client" coming in two years later claiming you undertook the case even though you never heard from the client again. Let there be no misunderstanding that you are doing nothing further until you receive the signed fee agreement and the check.

(22) *Clarify Any Loose Ends.* Give the client an opportunity to ask if anything is not clear.

(23) *Have the Client Sign the Fee Agreement, and Get Your Retainer for Fees and Costs.* Upon execution and return of the fee agreement, you have a client, and the client has a lawyer.

The Economics of Law Practice Section of the American Bar Association has published a book which may be helpful in expanding the scope of this chapter: *Legal Fees and Representation Agreements* (1983). It is available at $20.00 ($11.00 to members of the Section) from American Bar Association, Order Fulfillment 511, 750 N. Lake Shore Drive, Chicago, IL 60611.

Balancing the Public's Need for Legal Services and the New Lawyer's Need to Eat

Society as a whole has an obligation to provide legal services to those who need them. Lawyers as a part of society should bear their proportionate share of this burden.

There are some ignorant, misguided people (including some new lawyers) who feel that lawyers alone are obligated to bear the entire burden of society. This is not now, and never has been, the case.

The lawyer who feels that each lawyer is obligated to do free legal work for anyone who wants it should not go into private practice unless he or she can get a subsidy from some organization.

Ethical Considerations 2-16 and 2-26 state the situation as fairly as possible and are submitted here for your consideration.

"Financial Ability to Employ Counsel: Generally
EC 1-16 The legal profession cannot remain a viable force in fulfilling its role in our society unless its members receive adequate compensation for services rendered, and reasonable fees should be charged in appropriate cases to clients able to pay them. Nevertheless, persons unable to pay all or a portion of a reasonable fee should be able to obtain necessary legal services, and lawyers should support and participate in ethical activities designed to achieve that objective."

"Acceptance and Retention of Employment
EC 2-26 A lawyer is under no obligation to act as adviser or advocate for every person who may wish to become his client; but in furtherance of the objective of the bar to make legal services fully available, a lawyer should not lightly decline proffered em-

ployment. The fulfillment of this objective requires acceptance by a lawyer of his share of tendered employment which may be unattractive both to him and the bar generally."

Keep in mind that when a private practice lawyer does free legal work, another lawyer may be deprived of a job in a publicly funded agency.

I submit that private practice lawyers should earn a good income and then devote some portion of that income to activities which simultaneously provide work for other lawyers and provide lawyers for people who can't afford them.

I also believe that during the first few years the new lawyer should concentrate on building a solid financial basis for a practice so that in later years there will be resources available for charitable enterprises. If the new lawyer does not first build up a practice, there never will be a later time or later resources to devote to society as a whole.

How to Set Your Fees

No matter how long you practice law you'll make a lot of mistakes when you set fees. As a new lawyer you are obviously more vulnerable to making mistakes in fee setting than the more experienced lawyers.

There are no simple formulas for fee setting. Platitudes are plentiful and concrete advice is hard to come by. Acknowledging in advance my inability to give you a simple panacea, I'll try in this chapter to give you general rules for fee setting, emphasizing the problems you'll encounter in the early part of your career. Hopefully you won't quote $3,000.00 for a fee when you should have quoted a $300.00 fee, or vice versa.

Fee Surveys

The Economics of Law Practice committee or section of your state or local bar association probably conducts periodic surveys of prevailing fees being charged by firms for given types of work. These fee surveys are typically done by firm size. Bar associations don't like to disseminate these survey results for fear they will be equated with the old minimum fee schedules, which are generally not used any more. You may have to ask the Economics Chair of your bar association to get this information.

Other Lawyers

In my opinion the smartest thing you can do to get a handle on fee setting is to ask another lawyer. The other experienced lawyer will be able to give you some help in ascertaining the important factors which will affect fees and costs. If you explain to the other lawyer that you don't know what you are doing he or she will help you. Obviously you will get only generalizations. These generalizations are much better than nothing.

Contingency Fees

Contingency fees are common in some types of work such as personal injury and are absolutely prohibited in other areas such as criminal or domestic relations.

1. *Personal Injury—Auto Accident.* Fees are commonly quoted by formulas such as "one-third if no lawsuit is necessary or 40 percent if a lawsuit is necessary" or "one-fourth if settled before filing of suit or 40 percent if settled after suit is filed but before 30 days of trial date and 50 percent if tried or settled within 30 days of trial."

2. *Personal Injury—Assault and Battery.* Fees of 40 percent to 50 percent with a cash minimum fee of $300.00 to $600.00 paid in advance are common. Collection of judgments is difficult as there is often no insurance.

3. *Personal Injury—Slip Fall.* Fees of 45 percent to 50 percent are common due to difficulty of establishing liability.

4. *Personal Injury—Medical Negligence.* Usually slightly higher than personal injury auto accident due to high cost of preparation of case and difficulty of settlement until you are "on the courthouse steps."

5. *Workers' Compensation.* Depends on local practice. Private fee contracts not permitted or valid in some jurisdictions. A private fee agreement may even be illegal.

6. *Commercial Collections.* Usually 25 percent to one-third of collections, based upon amount involved.

Lump Sum Fees

This involves setting a lump sum fee regardless of how little or how much work is involved. This is very common in criminal matters and domestic relations. Although this method has the greatest potential for being grossly unfair to either the client or the attorney, it seems to be the most desired by clients who prefer a fixed fee. Since both you and the client will be relatively unsophisticated, this method is probably best for both of you.

A word of advice. If you grossly underestimated the fee, that's your mistake, not the client's. Continue doing the very best job you can on the case. When you finish the case tell the client what you should have charged. About one time in 25 a client will offer to pay the difference to bring the fee to the proper amount. Be careful not to suggest that the difference be paid. As with friends and relatives, the client has no way of knowing the value of the services unless you tell him or her. If you did $4,000.00 of work for $1,500.00, tell the client. The client should know the value of what has been received and that you're a person of your word. The client will respect you and use you again.

Minimum-Maximum Lump Sum Fees

For the new lawyer this method is also good when you can't get an accurate handle on the exact amount. Give the client a range of minimum to maximum. For example: "I cannot give you an exact fee quotation at this time since the amount of work required will depend upon how aggressively the other side fights. The minimum fee will be $150.00 and the maximum, to and including trial, will be $2,500.00."

Hourly Rates

I don't recommend the use of hourly rates in the first several months for new lawyers for two reasons:

1. The time you devote to a matter in many instances will be inordinate due to your inexperience. It's not unusual for something to take you 12 hours the first time, including research and drafting, because you are starting from ground zero. The seond time, using your form file as an aid, it may only take six hours; the third time perhaps only three hours and the fourth time one hour or less. There are many things I can do now in an hour or less which took me from 10 to 30 hours the first time I did it. Based on purely hourly rates the inexperienced lawyer will be more highly compensated than the more experienced lawyer.

2. You'll frighten the client away. It is difficult if not impossible to quote an hourly rate of $60.00 per hour to someone who earns $35.00 per day. There simply is no communication between you. If you estimate that the work should reasonably take 10 to 15 hours and you want $60.00 per hour, then tell the client the cost will be

between $600.00 and $900.00 and don't mention time.

Sophisticated business executives are used to being charged on an hourly rate; lower- and middle-class people are not used to paying on an hourly rate.

After you've been in practice six months or so you'll have enough background to be able to quote hourly rates where appropriate.

Fee by Stages

There will be cases where you simply cannot quote lump sum fees and where you don't want to quote hourly rates. You should try to break the work into "stages," estimating the work for each stage and then setting a fee for each stage as you go. An example would be as follows:

1. Research as to merits of case and written opinion: $350.00.

2. If I believe the case is meritorious and collectible, our fee will be one-third of recovery, giving you credit for $350.00 paid.

3. If I believe the case has uncertain merit or uncertain collectibility, you may use other counsel with no further obligation to us or you may proceed further as set forth.

4. Drafting of complaint: $275.00.

5. Law and motion appearances (prior to answer): $350.00 (includes two appearances if necessary; additional preparation and appearances $200.00 each if required).

6. Propounding or answering written interrogatories (four anticipated): each $100.00.

7. Deposition preparation and attendance: $200.00 per deposition of less than four hours, or $350.00 if more than four hours and less than ten hours.

8. Trial estimated (five days): $350.00 per day.

9. All other services not covered above: $60.00 per hour.

10. You may stop using our services at any stage simply by so notifying us. If we accept the case on a contingency basis and you subsequently discharge us, our fee will be the *greater* of one-third of any offers received prior to or within 5 days of being terminated or $60.00 per hour. If we decide not to proceed further after taking the case on a contingency, then you will have no further obligation past the $350.00 and out-of-pocket costs advanced.

Bonuses

I personally believe that fees should be related to results. I pay substantial bonuses to employees based upon money they earn for the firm or money they save the firm with management suggestions and secretarial productivity. I also believe in billing clients *over and above* the agreed hourly rate when we accomplish unusually good results for the client. On the other hand I sometimes reduce a fee *below* the agreed hourly rate when the results are poor for the client. I have rejected substantial fees based upon purely hourly compensation where the client was not agreeable to a bonus. I have refused to accept a case based on a purely hourly basis, where I would have earned between $25,000 and $50,000, because the client was not agreeable to a bonus of 10 percent of the amount saved. The amount in the case was in excess of $1,200,000, with another $300,000 in interest and penalties involved. I was not about to accept professional responsibility for $1,500,000 for 2 percent to 3 percent of the amount involved. I would have been happy to accept the fee arrangement if the amount involved had been about $500,000.

While the numbers involved here may be beyond what you can reasonably expect in your first year or two, the concept is the same for smaller amounts.

It goes without saying that the "bonus" must be agreed to in concept if not in exact amount as soon as possible in the case. The concept of a fee predicated in part upon the results obtained and the amount involved is recognized by DR 2-106(B)(4).

Setting Fees after the First Year or Two

After you've been in practice a year or two, much of the mystery in the fee-setting process will be removed, although some will always remain. You may wish to use different methods, examples of which follow (these methods are not necessarily recommended):

a. *Supply and Demand.* Charge all you can get in each case, subject to the fee not being unconscionable or "clearly excessive."

b. *Follow the Leader.* Charge what your contemporaries charge on the theory that they know what they are doing (a premise of doubtful reliability).

c. *Take What the Client Pays and Be Grateful.* This is a sure way to bankruptcy court (your personal bankruptcy). Remember that even churches doing the work of God have to close when their parishioners don't give enough.

    d. *Decide your own value:*

      1. Estimate the number of chargeable hours you work per year (Factor CH).

      2. Set the net dollar profit you wish to earn per year (Factor P).

      3. Estimate your overhead per year (Factor O).

      4. Hourly rate $= (P + O)$ divided by CH.

Legal Fees and the Code of Professional Responsibility

The Code of Professional Responsibility covers fees in Disciplinary Rule 2-106. Unfortunately, the code is of limited help to the new lawyer. It is very helpful in analyzing a situation in retrospect, but isn't very helpful to the new lawyer who wants to quote a fee to the client sitting across a desk.

I suggest you read DR 2-106 and try to apply it within the context of the suggestions in this chapter.

        "DR 2-106 *'Fees for Legal Services.'*

"(A) A lawyer shall not enter into an agreement for, charge, or collect an illegal or clearly excessive fee.

"(B) A fee is clearly excessive when, after a review of the facts, a lawyer of ordinary prudence would be left with a definite and firm conviction that the fee is in excess of a reasonable fee. Factors to be considered as guides in determining the reasonableness of a fee include the following:

    (1) The time and labor required, the novelty and difficulty of the questions involved, and the skill requisite to perform the legal service properly.

    (2) The likelihood, if apparent to the client, that the acceptance of the particular employment will preclude other employment by the lawyer.

    (3) The fee customarily charged in the locality for similar legal services.

    (4) The amount involved and the results obtained.

    (5) The time limitations imposed by the client or by the circumstances.

    (6) The nature and length of the professional relationship with the client.

(7) The experience, reputation, and ability of the lawyer or lawyers performing the services.

(8) Whether the fee is fixed or contingent.

"(C) A lawyer shall not enter into an arrangement for, charge, or collect a contingent fee for representing a defendant in a criminal case."

Should You Charge for the Initial Consultation?

Our firm does not charge separately for the first consultation. We feel that the public should not be afraid to see a lawyer when they want to find out if they need professional help. After we have gotten the facts we advise them that they do or that they don't require professional help. (See points 3 and 4 in sample fee representation letter in "The Fee and Representation Letter" chapter.) We include the initial consultation services in the first bill if we do further services for the client.

Other lawyers tell the prospective client to bring a check to the initial interview. I feel that demanding a fee in advance for the first consultation leaves the public and potential clients with the impression that the lawyer is more interested in making money than in helping the client.

I have no proof, but I feel that our method gives the clients respect and confidence and encourages candor in relating the facts. I also feel that the client understands that we are sincerely trying to help.

Don't Quote Fees or Give Legal Advice Over the Telephone to New Clients

In discussing charging for the initial consultation in the last chapter I said that some lawyers do ask the client to bring a check in advance of the initial interview, and that others don't require a check in advance of the initial interview. Both schools of thought have one thing in common, which is: *"Get the client into the office for the interview."*

Don't be seduced into the trap of quoting fees or giving legal advice over the phone. As a new lawyer you'll want to talk to a prospective client all you can to impress him or her with your legal knowledge and ability to handle the case.

Be wary of the "client" who won't come into the office for an appointment and who is trying to pump you for legal advice by telephone. In addition to pumping you for legal advice, such clients will continually try to get a price quotation over the telephone. When you ask these people how they got your name they'll typically be very vague. They'll say that someone—whose name they don't know—at a bank or at a party recommended you. They may claim there were referred by the bar association, but they'll never be recommended by any client you know of.

This type of person will absolutely refuse to come into the office even when you say there's no charge for the consultation. You'll get some story about being in town for a few hours or some other crazy excuse. When you ask for a phone number of address to contact him or her, you'll get another long story, giving neither address nor phone number.

This type of person has absolutely no interest in using you for a lawyer. He or she may have gotten your name from a phone book or some client who owes you money. In most instances this person already has a lawyer and is trying to use your advice and fee quotation to get the other lawyer to reduce a fee.

You are a fool if you give legal advice to this unknown voice over the telephone. When you get sued for malpractice two years later by this "voice" you'll have only yourself to blame.

Be firm. Tell the "voice" that you can't quote fees or give legal advice until *after* you've interviewed the client to be sure you have all the relevant facts and have examined the relevant documents. Don't waver. You'll be better off. If this person never comes, you won't have lost a client; you'll have lost a freeloading problem. It's hard to say "No" when you're a new lawyer who wants all the clients possible, but believe me, it's the best thing.

Getting Money Up Front
From New Clients

Abraham Lincoln is reputed to have said, "The lawyer should always get some part of his fee in advance from the client. In this way the client knows he has a lawyer and the lawyer knows he has a client."

Whether you call it a "retainer fee" or an "advance," or any other name, the concept is still the same. Before doing a significant amount of work for a new client, the lawyer should always obtain part, if not all, of the fee in advance. It is not fair to the client or the lawyer for the client to undertake legal services that he or she cannot afford. I advocate that it is better for the lawyer not to do the work and not get paid than to do the work and not get paid.

Most people who seek the services of a lawyer expect to pay. A responsible client will not start expensive litigation if it is known that you will have to stop work if the fee is not paid as agreed. The client who cannot afford to pay for the services is not likely to pay the retainer fee in advance, thus saving the lawyer a lot of unpaid work. The prospective client who asks, "Don't you trust me?" should be answered: "No, why should I? I don't know you yet. If I can't protect my own legal interests, then what kind of job could I do protecting yours?" The same client who would be angry or insulted over paying some money in advance is usually the one who will be angry and insulted over your bill after you have done the work.

I am *not* advocating that you not do pro bono public legal work or just plain free legal work for experience. I *am* saying that *you* and *not* the client should decide when you are going to do nonpaying legal work. Being the most-loved lawyer in town won't help when you are evicted from your home and have to list your secretary's salary on a bankruptcy. We are dealing with an economic issue.

Cash Fees

When a client offers you cash fees, call in a secretary to count the money and to give a receipt to the client. Deposit the cash intact in the bank with the deposit ticket indicating the source of the fee. Be very careful about the client who makes some sort of remark to the effect that the cash is "hot" or that he or she is not keeping any record of payment of the fee. When the client says that only two people will know, the two of you, tell the client that that's one too many, namely, him or her. This type of client is a good candidate to try to blackmail you at a later date. He or she will threaten to turn you in to the IRS if you press for an unpaid fee. Such a client may also threaten to turn you into the IRS unless you "loan" him or her money. When you get cash fees, go out of your way to let the client know that you've recorded the fees in your books and will report them in your income tax return. (As a new lawyer you won't have the problem of being in too high a tax bracket.)

Client Costs

The subject of cost advancement is subject to debate and disagreement in many jurisdictions. The purpose of this chapter is not to take any position, but to caution the new lawyer that you can go broke advancing costs. Costs should always be considered and handled from a cash flow point of view, keeping in mind your economic survival from a profit or loss point of view and also from a case acceptance or rejection point of view.

Never be afraid to ask an experienced lawyer what out-of-pocket costs and fees should be anticipated in a given type of case and at what stage of the proceeding they will have to be paid.

If at all possible, you should not have to finance client costs. You are not a bank or financial company. You should *always* ask the client for estimated costs in *advance* to place in your trust account to be used as needed and replenished as used. You should ask for costs in advance even in contingency fee cases.

The reality of life, however, is that you will be financing client costs for a number of reasons, such as:

1. Indigent client with meritorious case.

2. Convenience. You "lay out" the money for the client because it is more convenient, especially with smaller amounts such as long distance telephone calls, court fees, etc.

3. The competition. Other lawyers in your community don't ask for or get costs up front and you're afraid of losing the client if you insist.

In some cases you should *ask* the client for costs up front, but indicate to the client that if necessary or convenient, you can advance them subject to monthly reimbursement or reimbursement at the end of the case (meritorious accident cases, corporate formation, fee, etc.).

In some cases you shouldn't take the case unless the client puts the costs "up front" (slip falls, doubtful recovery cases, etc.)

In some cases the amount of costs required on a meritorious case is so large that neither you nor the client can afford the costs, in which case you should associate in a well-financed law firm that can advance the costs for cases that require large amounts of investigation or outside experts (antitrust, medical malpractice, etc.) and cases where the pretrial, the trial and the appeals will take years.

The Importance of Cash Up Front for Survival
(Also Known as "Foonberg's Rule")

The concept of "cash up front" is a critical one for two reasons:
1. The case selection process for all lawyers new and experienced.
2. Economic survival for new lawyers.

Foonberg's Rule of "cash up front" can also be stated in three additional ways:

1. The client who can't or won't pay you cash up front at the beginning of the case is the same client who can't or won't pay you cash during the case and is the same client who can't or won't pay you cash at the end of the case.

2. As I said earlier if you can choose between doing the legal work and not getting paid or not doing the legal work and not getting paid, you are better off not doing the work and not getting paid.

3. A bona fide client who seriously cares about his or her case will give you a cash advance for costs and/or fees to the best of their ability. A flaky client or one who is holding back on telling you everything will not advance cash on his or her own case because they know things either about the case or themselves that would affect your accepting or rejecting the case. (There will be some exceptions in criminal cases.)

How to Get Cash Up Front to Reduce Bad Debts and Increase Cash Flow and Avoid Going Under

As a practicing CPA, I quickly learned that the most common cause of new business failure is under-capitalization. Over the years, the statistics put out by the Small Business Administration bear this out. In other parts of this book, I have emphasized the importance of minimizing overhead and cash outlay in the beginning of your practice. I have also dwelled heavily on how to borrow money. I have also indicated the importance of the concept of cash up front (Foonberg's Rule) in the case selection process.

In this chapter, I will cover how to *use* the cash-up-front concept. Perhaps you will be able to modify these examples to fit your own situations. First, things you can say at the interview:

1. "Mr. Jones, it is office policy to ask new clients for a cash retainer. This retainer will be placed in a trust account and used for payment of fees and costs to other people. Each month we will send you a statement and will draw upon the trust account for payment of these fees and costs."

Alternative 1. "When we have used up the funds in the trust account, we will then bill you monthly and will expect you to pay upon receipt of the bill."

Alternative 2. "Each month we will expect you to send a check payable to the trust account to replenish the funds used."

2. "You can discharge me at any time and I will simply refund the unearned funds to you." (This reassures the client who is afraid you won't do the work after the funds are paid.)

Other things you can say and do:

1. "I tried to pay my secretary with accounts receivable, but the supermarket wanted cash from my secretary."

2. "Mr. Smith, you appear to have a meritorious case and I am willing to invest my time and overhead in your case and get paid my fee when the case closes, but I'm not a banker. I don't loan money to clients or anybody else. I expect you to advance $_____ to my trust account to be used for out-of-pocket costs. None of the money will go to me for fees, but I expect you to advance your own costs."

3. "Mr. Smith, neither you nor I want you to start the case, then have to abandon it or postpone it in the middle because you can't pay your bill. It's better for both of us for you to pay the legal fees in advance so you won't have to worry about it if you run out of money one or two years from now during the case."

There is no substitute for simply asking for the cash up front in a simple, forthright manner.

How to Word Invoices that Clients are Happy to Pay

The basic secret in invoicing is to tell the client everything you did. There is no such thing as an invoice that is too long. If you do a good job of preparing invoices, clients will think they're getting a bargain and will be glad to pay them before you reconsider how little you seem to be charging.

Source of Information for Invoices

The source of information for invoices is your time records. If you recorded everything you did, then preparing the invoice will simply be a matter of transferring the services rendered record from your time records to the invoices.

How to Word the Invoice

The most important thing in invoicing is to list every single *document* you prepared or reviewed. Clients often think that lawyers are in the stationery business. They ask, "How much for a will . . . or a partnership agreement . . . or a lease . . . or a lawsuit?" List every single letter, court form, document (including the number of drafts or revisions) which you worked on . Also indicate whether you reviewed the document or prepared it or revised it. Also list the forms your secretary prepared, including such documents as summonses, declarations or returns of service, and instructions to the clerk of court. Examples of three invoices are included at the end of this section.

Billing for Telephone Calls

Clients despise paying for telephone calls. Even our most sophisticated clients grit their teeth and mumble when charged for telephone calls. However, the same clients gladly and willingly pay for correspondence or other tangible "stationery."

When clients call and ask a question about legal rights in a given fact situation, they balk at paying for that advice. ("All I did was ask a simple question about mechanics' liens that didn't require any work" is a typical response to the bill.)

On the other hand, if you immediately send a letter repeating the facts given you and your opinion, the client will gladly pay for "correspondence and telephone conference concerning Mechanics Lien Law." As an added benefit, you decrease your malpractice exposure by repeating the given facts or questions in the event the client later claims he or she gave you different facts.

Show Dates of Services

Your invoice should show every single date you worked on the matter even if only a minor service was rendered on a particular date. A client will usually be impressed by the fact that you worked on his or her case on six or seven different dates during a month. This technique lets clients know you are giving their cases continual attention.

Do *NOT* list the date opposite the service rendered. List the dates at the end of the invoice. If you worked on a single document on two different dates, the client erroneously may think that you are double billing if you show the same or a similar description twice.

Show Litigation

If there is a pending lawsuit, always show the name(s) of the case(s), the court(s) where the matter is pending and the case number(s). Clients know that litigation is expensive (because you warned them at the inception of the matter), and by listing the court information you remind them monthly that the matter is expensive because litigation is expensive and not because you are expensive.

Don't Show Number of Hours of Service

Unless your fee agreement requires you to spell out the time devoted to each part of the work, don't do it. Listing each and every service and time often upsets the client over some minor aspect of the invoice.

If your fee agreement requires showing the hours worked, show the hours at the end of the invoice after all services are set out. Do not show every time detail alongside the work done unless the client asks for it.

Sample Invoices
Which invoice do you think your client would be most willing to pay?

Invoice 1

Re: Professional Services Rendered $450.00

Invoice 2

Re: Professional Services Rendered. Motion for Change of Venue and Answer to Complaint. $450.00

Invoice 3

Re: Professional Services Rendered. Jones vs. Smith, Los Angeles Superior Court Case No. 123456: Analysis of Complaint; office conference with Arthur Smith to obtain facts of case and to discuss stragety of defending; preparation of Motion for Change of Venue, including Notice of Motion for Change of Venue, Points and Authorities in Support of Motion, Declaration of Arthur Smith in Support of Motion; Declaration of Attorney in Support of Motion; preparation of Proposed Answer to Complaint; preparation of Declaration of Service by Mail of various pleadings. Telephone conference with Arthur Smith and opposing counsel concerning no settlement of case. Telephone conference with clerk of court and opposing counsel to obtain hearing date for Motion; preparation of Order Granting Change of Venue. (Services rendered January 4, 5, 7, 9, 11, 13, 15, 16, 25, 26, and 28, 19____.) $450.00

The Importance of
Monthly Billing

Invoices should be sent out monthly. You pay secretaries and clerks two to four times a month. You pay rent, telephone and bank loans monthly. You need income on a monthly basis. You cannot pay payables with work in process or accounts receivable. Monthly billing lets you match your income against your expenses.

Monthly billing lets the client know you are constantly working on his or her matter.

Monthly billing allows you to determine when a client cannot or will not pay a bill.

Clients prefer to make progress payments as the case progresses rather than be shocked with a big bill at the end of the case. You are not doing the client any favor by letting bills run up that can't be paid. If the client is not happy with the results of the case, there may be an unwillingness to pay the last bill.

If the client cannot pay legal fees "as you go," you should consider handling the case on a contingency fee basis. If you have a low opinion of the merits of the case or the collectibility and don't want to proceed on a contingency basis, then you should be fair to the client and try to dissuade him or her from the litigation. Encourage the client to seek other counsel who may disagree with you as to the merits or collectibility, and who will take the case on a contingency fee basis. If there is no possible recovery and a defense is necessary, the client should be directed toward an agency with publicly paid lawyers.

(See chapter on "Cases and Clients that Should be Turned Down.")

Final Billing on Completion of a Matter

Even though you have been billing your client monthly, there will be a final bill. This bill is usually a fairly large one because of the work normally incident to the conclusion of a legal matter. You will have put in a lot of time in trying the matter or in negotiating the settlement and drafting the documents.

There are two basic reasons for getting in the final bill as soon as possible after the matter is concluded:

A. *The client's financial condition.* Often the client is about to receive or pay a large amount of money as a result of the conclusion of the case. If the client is going to receive funds, you want to be paid before they are dissipated. If the client is going to pay the money (or go bankrupt), this may be your last chance to get paid.

B. *The Client's "Curve of Gratitude."* My version of the famous Client's Curve of Gratitude is based on an article in *Law Office Economics and Management* and is found on the following page. Obviously the time to send the bill is between points 8 and 9.

After studying the Client's Curve of Gratitude you'll understand the importance of sending a final bill when the matter is concluded.

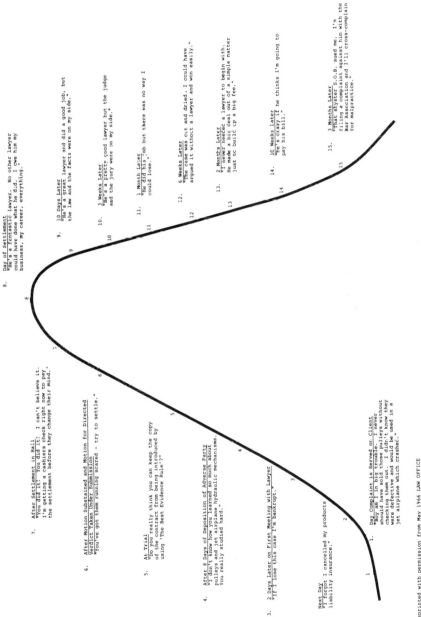

7. **After Settlement in Hall**
"You did it! You did it! I can't believe it. I'm getting a cashiers check right now to pay the settlement before they change their mind."

8. **Day of Settlement**
"He's a fantastic lawyer. No other lawyer could have done what he did. I owe him my business, my career, everything."

9. **10 Days Later**
"He's a great lawyer and did a good job, but the law and the facts were on my side."

10. **3 Weeks Later**
"He's a pretty good lawyer but the judge and the jury were on my side."

11. **1 Month Later**
"He did his job but there was no way I could lose."

12. **6 Weeks Later**
"The case was cut and dried. I could have argued it without a lawyer and won easily."

13. **2 Months Later**
"I never needed a lawyer to begin with. He made a big deal out of a simple matter just to build up a big fee."

14. **10 Weeks Later**
"He's crazy if he thinks I'm going to pay his bill."

15. **3 Months Later**
"That shyster S.O.B. sued me. I'm filing a complaint against him with the Bar Association and I'll cross-complain for malpractice."

6. **After Motion Sustained and Motion for Directed Verdict Taken Under Submission**
"You've got them running scared – try to settle."

5. **At Trial**
"Do you really think you can keep the copy of the contract from being introduced by using 'The Best Evidence Rule'?"

4. **After 8 Days of Deposition of Adverse Party**
"I don't know how you learned so much about pulleys and jet airplane hydraulic mechanisms. You really studied hard."

3. **2 Days Later on First Meeting with Lawyer**
"If I lose this case I'm bankrupt."

2. **Next Day**
"I forgot I cancelled my products liability insurance."

1. **Day Complaint is Served on Client**
"Boy am I in big trouble. I never should have sold those pulleys without checking them out. I didn't know they were defective and would be used in a jet airplane which crashed."

The Client's Curve of Gratitude

Reprinted with permission from May 1966 LAW OFFICE ECONOMICS AND MANAGEMENT published by Callaghan & Co., 6141 N. Cicero Ave., Chicago, Ill. 60646. ©1966 Callaghan & Co.

How to Make Clients Happy
to Pay Legal Fees
by Selling Them Stationery

Clients often have difficulty understanding that you are selling your professional advice. Professional advice is intangible. You can't see it or feel it; there is always a natural reluctance to pay for things that you can't see or feel. I have given this and similar advice in other parts of this book, because I feel the advice is important enough to be repeated.

Clients believe that lawyers are in the stationery business. They will ask you, "How much do you charge for a will . . . or a lease . . . or a lawyer's letter . . . or a lawsuit . . . or a partnership agreement?" Clients rarely ask you how much per hour you charge. Therefore, try whenever possible to convert your advice into stationery.

For example, a client calls and asks you a question about garage mechanic's liens. You tell the client that the mechanic at the garage has a lien on his or her car for up to $300.00 for parts and labor. If you send the client a bill for the telephone call for $10.00 you will get an angry response over being charged for a "telephone call." ("All I did was ask a simple question about mechanic's liens that didn't require any work," is a typical response to the bill.)

On the other hand, you should immediately send the client a letter repeating the facts given you, and your opinion. Send the client a photocopy of the applicable statute. He or she will gladly pay $35 for "correspondence and telephone conference concerning Mechanics Lien Law." As an added benefit the lawyer decreases (or increases) malpractice exposure by repeating the given facts or questions in the event the client later claims different facts were given.

Many clients save forever anything they receive from a lawyer. Make the client happy. Bombard him or her with copies of the paperwork.

134

Clients can understand paying for paperwork. They often can't understand paying for "advice." Send copies of checks, correspondence, pleadings, statutes, cases, etc. Clients want the paperwork and stationery and will pay for it.

What to Do *with* the Huge Fee

Occasionally, lawyers start their own law practice because of a single huge case which they can take with them from the old firm. I know of one lawyer who started his career with a $2.5 million fee on a single anti-trust case. (He tried the case and gave his old firm one-half of the fee.) I know of another lawyer who started his career with a probate case with a fee of over $1 million.

Even if you don't start your career with a huge fee, you may get one at some point in your practice. The whole world will stand in line to sell you tax shelters. At one time hustlers of tax shelters were promising 4-to-1 write-offs on oil wells and 6-to-1 write-offs on lithographs. I believe that for a high enough fee someone would have created a tax shelter package of a lithograph of an oil well with a resultant 24-to-1 write-off.

The safest, most secure, risk-free way, I know of to shelter as much income as possible, and still have the cash available, is through the use of a professional corporation and a corporate benefit plan.

If your motivation for starting your own law practice is a single huge fee, then I implore you to consult a competent tax lawyer before you do so.

How to Make Money by Reading Advance Sheets and Technical Journals

I spend about an hour a day reading advance sheets and journals for the following reasons:

1. To be a good lawyer by keeping current on the law;
2. To make money;
3. To impress clients that I care about them and their legal matters.

I read the journals with a red pen in hand. When I find an article or new case that affects or may affect a case in the office, I circle it and write the case name and client name on the face of the journal as well as the page number where the materials can be found. I then dictate a letter (you can do it the next day at the office or if, like me, you read advance sheets at home or on airplanes or during commuting, you can use a portable machine, as I do, to dictate it immediately.)

A sample letter would be as follows:

Ms. Mary Jones
123 Main Street
Hometown, USA

      RE: Jones vs. USA USDC Case #_____
      Smith vs. USA decided June 1, 198__

Dear Ms. Jones:

      I am enclosing a copy of the decision of the Second Circuit Court of Appeals in the case of *Smith vs. USA*. This case was decided on May 15 and was just reported in the May 25th, 19___ issue of the *Daily Journal*. A copy of the case is enclosed for your files.

      The facts and legal issue of the Smith case may have an

effect upon your case. The case was decided by the Second Circuit Court of Appeals in New York. We are in the Ninth Circuit here in Los Angeles, but nonetheless the Department of Justice (the trial lawyers for the government) will be aware of the case and it may affect the Judge's decision in your case.

You will note that one of the principal issues in the Smith case is the principal issue in your case (deduction of travel expenses for spouses).

No response on your part is necessary. We thought you would appreciate receiving this information.

Very truly yours,

Typical Client Costs

If you are handling a certain type of case for the first time or are not quite sure of yourself, ask an experienced attorney for help in estimating the kinds of costs to be anticipated in a given case. The costs listed here are simply some of the typical or "classic" costs you are likely to encounter in any given type of case.

Litigation

Police reports, court reporter minimum appearance fee, transcript costs, deposition appearance fees, medical examinations, medical opinions and reports, medical testimony, investigations, photocopy costs, record copying costs (employer and hospitals), expert opinion and testimony costs in addition to nonmedical, including accountants, actuaries, engineers, etc., Sheriff's fees or other process fees, and travel expenses.

Business Formation and Businesses Generally

Advance payment of franchise or income taxes, filing fees for Secretary of State or for County Clerk, permit fees for stock issuance, transfer taxes, certified copies, recording costs (per page), newspaper notices and advertising, stock certificate, corporate seals and books, notarial fees, travel costs, long distance telephone calls and telex costs, title searches and reports, and out-of-state attorneys.

Again, these are only typical costs to be considered and you should always, when necessary, ask for help from other attorneys in estimating costs.

Can You or Should You Pay or Receive "Forwarding Fees" or Referral Fees?

Can You Pay Such Fees?

To Lawyers?

As a general rule, you *can* pay or receive forwarding fees if you follow certain rules as set forth in Desciplinary Rule 2-107. These rules are as follows:

a. The client knows there will be a division of fees and consents. This consent should be in writing.

b. The total fee of the lawyers is no more than the reasonable value of what the client received. This is not usually a problem if the receiving lawyer charges a usual and customary fee and the lawyers share that fee. This restriction is intended to prevent overcharging the client to cover the fee splitting. For example, if a personal injury lawyer normally charges a contingency fee of 40 percent of recovery for a certain type of case, but increases the fee to 50 percent to cover the forwarding fee, then this fee conduct is probably improper.

c. There is a division in proportion to the services performed and the responsibility assumed by each. This is easier preached than practiced. I don't know how to divide responsibility proportionately. I suppose a written agreement between the two lawyers stating that they agree to divide responsibility proportionately is as close as you can come.

To Nonlawyers?

No, you may not. Fee splitting with nonlawyers is the second fastest way to get disbarred, running second after improper use of clients' funds. Fee splitting with nonlawyers is absolutely prohibited and there are no ifs, ands, or buts. Indirect fee splitting schemes are just as wrong as direct payments. Sample illegal fee splitting devices are: paying "investigators" a percentage of fees; paying "landlords" or "business managers" a percentage of fees.

Should You Pay or Receive Such Fees?

From a purely economic, short-range point-of-view, forwarding fees may be a very desirable policy for a young lawyer for the following reasons:

1. It encourages getting the client over to a qualified specialist rather than leaving the client with an inexperienced lawyer who is afraid to lose a fee.

2. On an hourly rate, both the sending and receiving lawyer get relatively well compensated at no increase in price to the client. This is particularly true in percentage and standard fee situations. The specialist can accomplish the task in fewer hours and will get the fees more quickly.

From a long-range economic point-of-view, referring clients to others may be detrimental to the growth of your practice, since you've given up the major portion of your fee and since the client may refer other clients to the specialist rather than to you. Although a receiving lawyer should decline to accept employment on other matters from a previously referred client, this restriction does not apply to the people the client refers.

To illustrate: Suppose Ms. Client comes to you, Mr. Swellperson, with a case, and you refer Ms. Client to Mr. Specialist, who satisfactorily handles the matter. Two years later Ms. Client calls Mr. Specialist on an unrelated matter. Mr. Specialist should refer Ms. Client back to you rather than accepting the employment. In theory, this is simple. In practice, it often does not work. Ms. Client will usually say something along the line of, "I don't want to go back to Mr. Swellperson. It's you I have confidence in. If you won't accept my case, then I'm going to a third lawyer because I don't want to go back to Mr. Swellperson"; or the conversation may be to the effect, "I don't want Mr. Swellperson because he didn't want me." However you dress the package, the results are the same: Mr. Swellperson never sees the client again nor does he see the people referred by the client. Whether this result is good or bad or right or wrong is beyond the scope of this book.

Is There an Acceptable Middle Ground?

I believe there is an acceptable middle ground that is fair to the client and fair to you. I engage a specialist to work for me. I pay the specialist by the hour out of my own funds to get advice on how to handle the case and upon the merits or value of the case. Often the specialist has no contact with the client at this point. The specialist should be paid a consultation fee "up front" by you and then be given the facts by you. The specialist will tell you if he or she thinks the case can be handled by you with assistance, or if the matter is so far over your head that both you and the client would suffer if you tried to handle the matter without the assistance of a specialist.

For example, products liability cases or aircraft crash cases may require tens of thousands of dollars for investigators and testing. A difficult medical malpractice case may require expertise possessed by few lawyers. A first-degree murder case is no place to get some experience before a criminal jury. There are many types of cases where you simply will not have the bankroll or expertise to handle a case simply because it's too big or too complicated.

On the other hand, if you can handle the case with the help of a paid specialist, you will have the best of all worlds in that you will still earn the major part of the fee, keep a well-served client and his or her referrals, and receive experience under expert tutelage.

In the Final Analysis, Should You Pay the Referral Fees?

On balance, during the first year of your practice, you should pay referral fees as asked for. Referrals from other lawyers can be a significant source of cases, experience and fees in the beginning of your career. The case you get from the other lawyers will not be any bargain from a fee point-of-view, but if you play it straight and honest with the referring lawyer, he or she will gain confidence in your integrity and refer more cases to you. In most cases, the referring lawyers who send you the low-pay cases will *not* want a referral fee, but they might, and if so, pay it following the rules set forth in Disciplinary Rule 2-107.

Caveat

As a general rule, neither courts nor legislatures are concerned about fights between lawyers over fees.

The advice I have given here is general advice. It behooves you to make inquiry of local lawyers to modify this general advice to your local situation. The rules and law in this are changing rapidly, and you must be sure you are current. Some of this advice may be totally inapplicable to your local situation and, in fact, may even lead to unethical conduct judged by local standards.

"Bedside Manner" in Setting Fees

A. *Be Firm.* No matter which method of setting fees you use, be firm. If you are uncertain or wishy-washy, clients will rapidly lose confidence in you as a potential lawyer to handle their cases. After all, if you can't set a value on your own services, perhaps they have no value.

B. *Use Words Like "Per My Standard Fee" or "The Standard Fee" or "In Cases Like This."* Instill confidence in the client.

C. *Don't Ask the Client What the Fee Should Be.* This is one way to guarantee the client's using another lawyer.

D. *Distinguish Between Uncertainty in the Amount of the Fee and Uncertainty in the Manner of Setting the Fee.* When it is impossible because of the facts in the case to tell the client what the legal services will cost in total, you can still confidently set the method of computing the fee.

E. *Don't "Back Down."* If you quote "one-third" or "$60.00/hour" or "$750.00 " for the matter, don't back down when the client suggests one-fourth or $50.00/hour or $500.00 for the matter. If you back down, the client will think you were deliberately attempting to overcharge. The same client will again try to get a discount as a precondition to letting you close the case. What you look upon as an accommodation will be taken as a symbol of overcharging or dishonesty.

F. *Don't Be Swayed by What the Client Says Another Lawyer Charges.* Usually there is no other lawyer, or if there is or was another lawyer, the client had no confidence in that person. Clients who really want to use another lawyer wouldn't be seeing you.

G. *Don't Be Tempted by the Client Who Wants You to Take a Case at a Reduced Fee with the Promise of More Cases Later at Reasonable*

Fees If You Do a Good Job on the First Case. Take my word for it that there will be no later cases. Simply tell this client that in your office every piece of work has to stand on its own and pay its own way. Say that high-quality work can't be handled at low-quality fees, and if price is a principal consideration, you're wasting each other's time.

Put yourself in the position of a patient getting a filling. You ask the price. The dentist says, "My standard fee is $25." You state that you'll pay $15. The dentist says, "O.K." Aren't you going to be concerned about the quality of the filling you'll get?

H. *Be Sure You Bring up Fees at Your First Meeting.* (Note I said meeting—not phone call or letter.) Tell the client that you wish to discuss fees and that the client should never be embarrassed or ashamed to discuss fees with you. Don't leave the client wondering if you use a Ouija board to set fees.

I. *Suggest When Appropriate That the Client Borrow the Fees from a Credit Union or Relative.* When the client says he or she doesn't want to go to relatives, watch out. That person may not want to go to relatives because there is no intent to pay.

J. *Suggest, When Appropriate, That the Client Give You Collateral or Security for Payment of the Fees.* This is extremely important when the client may be defunct, bankrupt or jailed if the case is lost.

Remember, you can't have all the legal business in your state. Don't be overly concerned when a client goes to another lawyer for no other reason than cheaper fees. In these cases it is your gain and the other lawyer's loss. Be pleased that a client who was more interested in price than quality went elsewhere.

In summary, when discussing legal fees, you should exude confidence at every stage and be firm. Remember, if you can't properly represent your interests, the client will not think much of you.

When and How to Withdraw
from a Nonpaying Matter

In this chapter, I am limiting my discussion to the aspects of withdrawal due to payment factors. I recommend very highly to you Disciplinary Rules 5-102, 5-105, 2-109 and 2-110 of the Code of Professional Responsibility which cover withdrawals for other reasons such as conflict of interests, the attorney's being a witness, etc.

To paraphrase a line from a popular play, "Poverty may not be a shame, but that doesn't mean it's necessarily a blessing." Don't let a client take you under, too. Get out when it is in the best interest of both you and the client.

Whether you call it "dropping the case" or "withdrawing from the matter," the end result is the same. The desired result is that you are no longer taking a financial bath and the client is free to make some other lawyer rich (or poor).

If you are unhappy with the economic arrangements for the case or the client, you are going to have difficulty psychologically observing the Ethical Considerations which require you to *represent a client with zeal*. It should be obvious that if you like feeding your spouse and family, you may handle the paying cases and clients first, pushing the no-pay and poor-pay cases to the bottom of the pile where they may languish to the mutual detriment of both you and the client.

There are three possibilities with respect to withdrawing from a matter:

1. You cannot withdraw. (You are stuck.)
2. You must withdraw.
3. You should withdraw.

You Cannot Withdraw from a Matter

As a general rule, there are two instances when you cannot withdraw from a matter.

a. *The client has paid your agreed fee in full.* In this case, you have no recourse but to honor your fee agreement. You may not like the situation. If you erred in setting your fee, that's your problem. Chalk up your mistake as a learning experience. The next time a similar matter comes in, you'll have learned what a proper fee quotation should be.

You can sometimes get out of this mess by offering to refund 100 percent of the fees received. (Note: I said 100 percent — not some or part.) You should also offer to turn over your file to the client or to another lawyer.

Misunderstanding a fee arrangement is common with new lawyers because of their negligence in not putting the fee agreement in writing. I blame the lawyer, not the client, for misunderstandings. There is no excuse for misunderstandings.

b. *Your withdrawal would prejudice the client's case.* Although there are a few exceptions, you may not withdraw from a case unless you have taken appropriate steps to protect your client's rights. Oversimplified, you can't abandon your client on the courthouse steps a few hours before trial just because you haven't been paid. As above, if you allowed yourself to get stuck in this situation, you should grin and bear it. (See Disciplinary Rule 2-110(A)(2).)

You Must Withdraw

There are many times when you must withdraw from a case and these will be listed here. The problem from a financial point-of-view is whether or not you'll get paid for what you've done. As a very general oversimplification, you'll have a right to payment where the reason for the withdrawal is not your fault. If the reason for the withdrawal could have been, or should have been, foreseeable by you, then you probably won't get paid. In fact, DR 2-110(3) may require you to refund what you've collected in fees.

The following is a "warning list" of situations where you may have to withdraw from the case after you've started working ("Forewarned is forearmed."):

a. *You intend to call yourself as a witness for your client's case.*

b. *You will have a financial interest adverse to your client.* To a certain extent, all fee agreements are to some degree financially adverse to the client. This "adverse financial interest" problem is overcome if the client understands the situation and consents to it. You should protect yourself by getting the consent in writing when feasible.

c. *There is a conflict between two or more clients.* This problem can be solved by the client consenting to the continued employment.

d. *You know, or should know, you are not competent to handle the matter and will not associate with a competent lawyer.* Disciplinary Rule 6-101 is a new area of extension of legal ethics. Under the old Canons, competence was not considered an ethical matter. Under the Code a lawyer must associate with a competent lawyer when he or she is not competent to handle a matter.

e. *The client's case has no merit whatsoever and is being maintained for some ulterior motive such as delay or harassment.*

f. *Your conduct in handling the case would either be illegal or prohibited under the Disciplinary Rules.*

g. *You are fired.* The most obvious situation where you should withdraw is when you've been discharged as the lawyer. This raises the question of fees. In fixed fee and hourly fee cases, you probably will be entitled to be paid in full for what you've done.

In cases where you've been paid in advance, you will have to refund some portion of the fee unless you and the client have agreed that the fee was a *minimum* retainer and that you earned it by accepting employment in the case.

In contingency cases, how much you're entitled to depends on the law in your jurisdiction. In some jurisdictions, you will be entitled only to *quantum meruit* recovery. In some jurisdictions, you'll be entitled to the contingency percentage on whatever offers you've already received on the case. In some jurisdictions, you'll be entitled to your contingency percentage on the final settlement obtained in the case, even though obtained by another lawyer or the client in "pro per."

Local Custom and Rules

In some jurisdictions and tribunals, you cannot be relieved as the attorney for a corporation unless there is another lawyer willing to accept the case. This situation is created because corporations cannot represent themselves but can only be represented by an attorney licensed to practice law. Keep this in mind when you undertake the representation of a corporation.

In some jurisdictions, you cannot be relieved in a criminal case once you have appeared. This is a throwback to the days before the extensive public defender system existed. In those days, private lawyers simply did work for free as a professional obligation that public defenders and other government-paid lawyers now do for salaries. Some judges, trying to avoid more work for overburdened public defenders, insist on a private lawyer continuing on the case for free. Fortunately, this practice is disappearing, and judges now let unpaid private lawyers "off the hook" and request the paid lawyers to take on the case.

Unfortunately, you are going to learn a lot of lessons the hard way. There are many areas of practice where you just can't get "off the hook" without your client's help. Divorce court, bankruptcy court, cases involving children or decedents or incompetents are typical situations. You will find that your client has disappeared, you haven't been paid and you can't get out of the case. It's a real nightmare that will happen to you sooner or later in spite of the warnings of this book.

You Should Withdraw

In my opinion, you should withdraw from a case as soon as clients give you the indications that they're not going to live up to their fee agreement. Disciplinary Rule 2-110(C)(1)(f) specifically allows a lawyer to withdraw from a case when the client "deliberately disregards an agreement or obligation to the lawyer as to expenses or fees."

It is a basic rule of money management reinforced by the famous "Prudent Person" dicta of your law school days that losses should be cut short and not allowed to roll on. It is better for you (and your bank account) to lose out on three month's work on a nonpaying client than to lose out on six month's work. Cut your losses short. Take the time you would have spent on the nonpaying client and devote it instead to your paying clients.

How to Withdraw from a Case

The best way to withdraw from a case is to do so cleanly, honestly, and with as much advance notice in writing to the client as possible. A series of letters would set the stage for your subsequent motion to be relieved or substituted out. The letter should contain language to the following effect:

Letter No. 1.

Dear Client:

I cannot effectively represent a client when I have an overriding concern about being paid. In our written fee agreement, you promised to pay monthly as billed. My secretary has called twice to see if there is a problem or a mistake and you indicated that "a check is in the mail." You are now three months delinquent in paying your bill. Unless you pay the bill in full within the next ten days or make a new arrangement satisfactory to both of us, I shall have to terminate our professional relationship. I prefer to keep you as a client, but you will remember that when the case first arose, we discussed a fee agreement and put it in writing to make clear our arrangement. At that time, I was not willing to take the case on a contingency basis or on the basis of being paid at the end of the case. Nothing has happened to change that position. Please contact me within ten days.

Letter No. 2

Dear Client:

You have not responded to my letter of _____, a copy of which is enclosed. We no longer wish to be professionally responsible for your case and request you to seek other counsel. Please be assured that we will cooperate with your new attorney. Your trial date is about one year away, and you and your new attorney will have plenty of time to take reasonable measures to complete the trial preparation.

Letter No. 3

Dear Client:

We are enclosing a substitution-of-attorney form for you to sign where indicated by the red "X." We will file it with the court and will no longer be your attorneys in this matter. You will be your own attorney until you select another attorney. Upon receipt of the signed form, we will forward your files on to you.

Letter No. 4

Dear Client:

Enclosed is a copy of our motion to be relieved as attorneys in this matter. It will be heard _____, 19__, at 10:00 a.m. in room 123 of the Courthouse located at 5th and Elm. If our relief is granted, we will no longer be your attorneys, and you will be representing yourself until you select another attorney.

Letter No. 5

Dear Client:

Judge Jones granted our motion on _____, 19__. A copy of the order is enclosed. Effective immediately, we are not your attorneys in this matter. Your files have been sent under separate cover, "return receipt requested." We caution you to obtain new counsel as rapidly as possible to prepare your case for trial.

What Not to Do

Disciplinary Rule 2-110(C)(1)(f) specifically gives you the right to withdraw from the case where you are not paid. You *do not* have the right to keep the case and the client and refuse to do the work the case requires until you are paid. Therefore, you cannot, for example, refuse to proceed with a case until you are paid. You must either do what is required even though you are not being paid or you must withdraw from the case.

Part VI
Managing the Law Office

Management of the Law Office — General Comments

There are many gimmicks or tricks advocated by management experts for making the most effective use of your day. These suggestions run the gamut from that of training yourself to go to the toilet only during nonoffice hours to suggestions on how to dictate, where to place lighting, use of computers, etc.

Some of these suggestions are adaptable to law offices and some are not. I leave it to the reader to select his or her own management experts, books, consultants, etc.

The management suggestions I have made in this section and throughout this book are suggestions that I recommend to the new lawyer in practice based upon my experience.

Most of the suggestions are those that you will be able to use during your entire legal career, regardless of the size or nature of your practice or how long you've been in practice.

Overhead control and management of your office is to a great extent simply a matter of self-control and self-management in your first few years. Later you will have to control and manage others.

The difference between earning "a living" and earning "a good living" from the same practice will depend on how well you follow the lessons of this section on management.

Organizing Your Day to Make More Money

The president of one of America's "Big Three" auto manufacturers supposedly comes into his office every morning and stares out the window for a few minutes. Then he turns around to his desk and begins a list of "Things to Do." He puts the most important thing at the top and the list continues with things of decreasing importance.

If he only does one thing all day, he does the first thing on the list. After days or weeks he may take that last thing off the list by either ignoring it or giving it to someone else to do. He may *never* get to the last item on the list.

I don't know if this story is true or false, but it makes sense.

In hospital emergency rooms, sometimes several people arrive at the same time. This often happens after a large accident such as a multiple auto accident, building collapse or train wreck. There often are only one or two doctors then on duty to handle a large number of emergencies. Decisions are made to rank the medical cases in order of priority. Red blankets are put on those who can be saved but require immediate attention, purple blankets are put on those who will be saved if they are taken care of later. White blankets are given to those who really don't need emergency medical care to begin with and also to those who are going to die anyway—or who require so much attention that many others would die if they were taken care of. These cases are quietly wheeled out of the emergency room and given pain killers and ignored until the red blanket and purple blanket cases are taken care of. (The blanket color code differs from hospital to hospital, but the principle is the same.) Just as the auto executive and the hospital emergency room have to organize their work load, you have to organize yours.

156

I recommend starting each morning with a list of "Things to Do." Whether you use a plain legal pad or a commercially prepared pad is immaterial. The important thing is to discipline yourself to make a list and use it. The examples which follow this chapter, along with an explanatory note, should convey the idea. You might wish to review your list at fixed intervals such as lunch time, end of day, etc.

Things to do TODAY

DATE _December 1_

1	Call Bob Wilkins re program
2	Call Tom Peters re overdue bill
3	Answer attorney Smith's letter re Settlement
4	Have Mary call re stationery delivery
5	Start research on Jones case
6	Get accident report to Jones case
7	Start research on Alaska statute re employee liability
8	
9	Work on 9th circuit brief (due Feb 15)
10	Start research on Tax Article for Bar Journal (due Mar 1)
11	Get exhibit in auto damage in Evans case
12	
13	
14	
15	
16	
17	
18	
19	
20	

1. Beginning of day

Things to do TODAY

DATE _December 1_

1	Call Bob Wilkins re program
2	Call Tom Peters re overdue bill
3	Answer attorney Smith's letter re Settlement
4	Have Mary call re stationery delivery
5	Start research on Jones case
6	Get accident report to Jones case
7	Start research on Alaska statute re employee liability
8	
9	Work on 9th circuit brief (due Feb 15)
10	Start research on Tax Article for Bar Journal (due Mar 1)
11	Get exhibit in auto damage in Evans case
12	
13	Serve summons on Mr. Peters
14	Send the letter to Mr. Ramos
15	Get Tom to help on Tax Article
16	Set deposition of Mr. Fisk
17	Order the Peterson ground by new statute
18	
19	
20	

2 and 3. During the day

Things to do TODAY

DATE December 2

	✓	☐
1	Get accident reports on Jones case	
2	Serve summons on Mr. Peters	
3	Send fee letter to Mr. Thomas	
4	Start research on Jones case	
5	Arrange attorney, Smith, Deflin v. Settlement	
6	Set deposition of Mr. Fish	
7	Decide if Peters assignment by new statute	
8	Work on 9th amendment brief (due Feb 15)	
9	Start research on Tax Article for Bar Journal	
10	Ask Tom to help on the Tax Article	
11		
12		
13		
14		
15		
16		
17		
18		
19		
20		

4. End of day

Explanation

1. Start with a list of things to do. Put the most important thing at the head of the list. This should be the one thing you want most to get done during the day. Continue the list in order of descending importance.

2 and 3. Cross off things as you do them. Add new things which came up during the day.

4. Rearrange the list for the next day.

Organizing Your Desk to Make More Money

You will spend many hours at your desk. Your desk is not just a place to put ashtrays. It is the place where you will earn much of your living. You can make money at it.

1. Get a picture of your loved one(s) and place it on your desk facing *you*, not facing the client. Look at the photo whenever you feel awkward about charging fees. This photo will make it much easier to discuss fees, or to refer the client with no funds to legal aid. Update the photo when appropriate (e.g., when your children start to walk and then remind yourself that shoes cost money). Your family's growth will remind you of increased food needs. If you don't have a family, put up a picture of whatever is dependent on you, whether it be a boat or a plane or a pair of skis.

2. Put a clock on your desk facing you. A battery-operated, digital clock silently reminds you that time is a "wasting asset." (Use a battery-operated clock to avoid untidy electric wires all over your desk.) Put the clock squarely in front of you. Get in the habit of looking at it as soon as the phone rings, or the client comes in.

3. Put your telephone on the left side of your desk (if you are right-handed), so that you'll be able to dial or hold the phone with your nonwriting hand. Use a speaker phone so that you can use your hands to flip through a file when necessary.

4. Put your pen set on the right. Pick up your pen the moment you begin a telephone call or conference.

5. Your dictating microphone should be readily available on your desk.

6. Your time record book should be directly in front of you in the 2:00 o'clock position, in front of your pen so that you can jot down the

client's name when you pick up the pen; and add the services rendered when you put the pen back at the conclusion of the call or conference.

7. Keep a "Things to Do" pad. You can either buy a preprinted pad entitled "Things to Do," or just keep a list on any lined tablet. Every morning (or evening if you prefer), make a list of "Things to Do" and number them in order of importance. During the day, add the new things to the list as they come in and cross things off as they get done.

Prepare the list so that if you only did one thing all day, it would be the number one item. Don't be upset if it takes a long time to get to do the least important things, or if the least important things never get done (within limits of good sense and professional responsibility).

8. Files and papers neat on desk vs. cluttered desk:

This is another area where five lawyers have at least ten opinions. I have seen articles prepared by psychologists which indicate that a cluttered desk is psychologically debilitating to the lawyer, creating a subconscious dread and resistance to the amount of undone work. Supposedly, according to these articles, the client will feel that you are "too busy" to give personal attention, and will not hire you.

On the other hand, my desk looks like a rummage sale. Once a client refused to trust me with documents for fear they would get lost in the piles on my desk.

On some occasions, I have apologized to clients for my cluttered desk, and they have remarked that they want a lawyer who has lots of clients and work, and that they wouldn't want a lawyer who had very little work to do.

To me, a cluttered desk is a security blanket. When I see all the files, I don't worry that the phone won't ring that day.

This is an area where you should do whatever makes you feel comfortable.

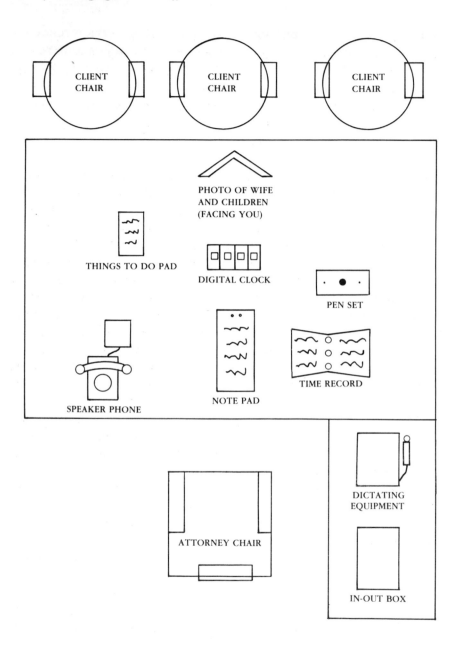

**Organizing Your Desk to Make Money
(Designed for a Right-Handed Lawyer)**

How to Keep Time Records
to Make More Money and
to Preserve Evidence of Work Done

The famous Missouri Bar Survey shows that lawyers who keep time records earn 40 percent more than lawyers who don't. Recent studies indicate that lawyers who keep *good* time records earn 15 percent more than lawyers who keep poor time records.

If you are concerned enough about earning a decent living to read this book, you are probably already keeping time records.

Whatever system or method you use, be sure you keep the time book or time slips on your desk in front of you as a constant reminder. There are many systems on the market. The Day Timer System is adequate for most sole practitioners. When I first started out, I used the Day Timer Junior book. After a few years, I "moved up" to the Day Timer Senior Sample Sheets. (Illustrations follow this chapter.)

Time records are not just billing records; they are, or can be, evidence for a claim in the estate when your client dies.

Record All Services

Record *all* telephone calls and all correspondence. If you decide later not to bill for a telephone call or letter, you can consider the services rendered as your contribution to the client. If you do not immediately record the services rendered, you will not be able to remember later to charge. It's simply not possible to remember what you did at the end of the month or the end of the week or even the end of the day.

Allow No Exceptions

Record *all* services rendered. If you are selective, you will tend to err towards not recording enough.

Don't Wait

Pick up your pen with your right hand when you pick up the phone with your left hand. Write the name of the client when you start the call or letter or conference and record the service the instant you hang up the phone or finish dictating the letter or returning from an out-of-office meeting or court appearance.

Time vs. Billing Records

You are keeping *time* records, not billing records. By recording all time, you will be able later to charge as appropriate, using hindsight. If you attempt to record only those services which at the time seem chargeable, you'll omit a lot of billable services. Remember, you are keeping time records, not billing records.

Review Your Time Records at the End of Each Day

Do not leave the office until you have added up your time for the day. If you come in at 9 a.m. and leave at 5:30 p.m. with an hour for lunch, you should have seven and one half hours of time recorded.

Time Records as Evidence

We keep time records for all work, including personal injury and worker's compensation. We have asked for and received fees based on time and services from various administrative agencies such as Worker's Compensation Boards, as well as from courts when submitting minors' cases for approval. Our time records have served as evidence in disciplinary proceedings brought against other lawyers; our records of telephone conversations with the other lawyers save them because their clients accused them of neglecting a case.

Time Records to Support Income Tax Deductions

You should record your out-of-pocket expenses immediately. Parking lot fees, public telephones, deductible meals and promotional expenses should be immediately recorded as the contemporaneous records required by the Internal Revenue Service.

21

FRIDAY
NOVEMBER,

OCTOBER	NOVEMBER	DECEMBER
	SUN MON TUE WED THU FRI SAT	
1 2 3 4	1	1 2 3 4 5 6
5 6 7 8 9 10 11	11th MONTH 2 3 4 5 6 7 8	7 8 9 10 11 12 13
12 13 14 15 16 17 18	9 10 11 12 13 14 15	14 15 16 17 18 19 20
19 20 21 22 23 24 25	16 17 18 19 20 21 22	21 22 23 24 25 26 27
26 27 28 29 30 31	23 30 24 25 26 27 28 29	28 29 30 31

40 Days Left

ITEM NO. TO BE DONE TODAY (NUMBER EACH ITEM)

1

NOTES & MEMOS MADE TODAY

SAN FRANCISCO EXPENSES Thursday 20 Nov
Cab from airport   9.75
Cab from district court to 9th Circuit   2.00
Cab back to district court   2.00
Photo copies and registration fees   7.75
airport back to airport   1.75
Parking LAX   3.00
                                        $26.25

21 Nov   Trip
Parking at El Ropoff   1.00
Fall to office for missing   15
Parking lot at Sunday Nov/Nov   3.00 $5.15
Parking at UCLA   1.00
Lunch at El Ripoff   38.00   charged on credit card

APPOINTMENTS & SCHEDULED EVENTS

NAME	PLACE	IN RE:	HOURS
			8 00 15 30 45
Mr. Chan re 9th Circuit 8:30 A			
			9 00 15 30 45
Conf John Cohen has @ 10 re Sweetheart			**10** 00 15 30 45
			11 00 15 30 45
Conf & lunch with Mr. Buske – start here @ Noon lunch @ 12:30 at El Ripoff			**12** 00 15 30 45
Bashr appointment @ 2:00			**1** 00 15 30 45
			2 00 15 30 45
			3 00 15 30 45
Meeting at North Coast @ 4:00PM			**4** 00 15 30 45
			5 00 15 30 45
7:30 – UCLA Law School – Program			**NIGHT HOURS**

SERVICES PERFORMED TODAY

325th Day • NOVEMBER, **FRIDAY 21**

HOURS	File/# Client	For/Party	In Re:/Parties	Description of Services	HRS 1/10
8	CARA INC			Conference with client re filing of brief and stay with 9th Circuit in San Francisco on Thursday 20 November	3/ 1/
9	Bala	US Franchise Tax Board		Letter to client with explanation of regulation # 68-462 as applied to case	1/2
	Cara Inc			Telephone Call with US atty re stay of execution	1/4
10	Sweetbread Inc			Telephone Conf with client re stay of execution	1/4
				Conf. John Cohen, CPA re depreciation possibilities for trucks	3/ 1/
	Bangkok Properties			analysis of 30% withholding requirements on interest remitted	1/2
11	Sweetbread, Inc			Memorandum to file re possible application of IRC Sect 269	1/2
	Calif Bank	US. Thomas		Speed letter to client re renewing judgment	1/4
12	Client Relations			Lunch with Mr. Brooks at El Ripoff Restaurant re possible representation	1 1/2
1	Brazilian Trade Assn.			Telephone call from Mr. Jones re proxies for meeting	1/4
	JCF Personal			Haircut at Barber Shop	1/
2	Jones adv. Smith			Telephone Call from Mr. Jones with preliminary facts and to set up meeting in office on Monday	1/4 a/c
	Sweetbread, Inc			Conference at offices of Lessa Northeast Co with Sam Peters and William Smith outside counsel for NE and Tom Jones House Counsel	
3				for NE and R H Samuels Controller for NE and William Arthur President of NE and Tom Goodguy President of Sweetbread	2
4				re possibility of arranging sale terms to write avoidance of 269 problem	
	Republic	Selbeck		Ltr to client summarizing results of meeting	1/2
5	Pants	adv. Pants		Conference client re doing research and getting facts to determine liability	
				Telephone call client at home Thursday night re set up meeting	1/4 n/c
	Bar Association			Telephone call from Tom Goodguy re my nomination for Trustee ship	1/4
NIGHT HOURS	Continuing Education			CEB program at UCLA on tax aspects of divorce and adoption	2
				TOTAL	10 3/4

PRINTED IN U.S.A.

How to Interview a Client

The way you conduct your interview will have a profound effect on whether or not the client has confidence in you and whether or not you will be engaged. Often the interview is the only face-to-face contact you have with your client unless you go to court. In this age of good telephonic and postal communications, subsequent client contact is often not face to face.

In the Reception Room

1. Be sure there are some straight-back chairs. Injured or elderly clients can't get into or out of plush or overstuffed sofas and chairs.

2. If the client is early, have the receptionist offer the client coffee or a soft drink. As an international lawyer, I have met with clients and lawyers all over the world, in such places as Peking, Rio, Tokyo, Cairo, Nairobi, Hong Kong, Istanbul, Geneva and London, among other places. It is an international custom appreciated by clients to offer them something to drink to "wet the whistle." Your client will be put in a relaxed mood by the beverage.

Be Prompt

Don't be early or late. If you have a 10 a.m. appointment, go in to get the client at 10 a.m., not 9:55 or 10:05. The client may take tardiness as a sign of disrespect (I do), or earliness as a sign of nothing to do.

Greet the Client

Ask, "Ms. Smith?" Don't assume that the only person in the reception room is your client. Your client may have gone to the toilet or back to move the car. If the person says, "Yes," then introduce yourself. Offer your hand in a handshake and say, "I'm John Jones." Don't introduce yourself as Mr. Jones, or Attorney Jones, unless this is the custom in your community. Calling oneself "Mister" or "Ms." is often taken as a sign of lack of self-confidence. The client knows you're a lawyer or he or she wouldn't be there.

Help the Client

If the client has a purse or coat or envelopes or documents, take it upon yourself to help carry the burdens.

Take Command of the Situation

From this point on, you must take command of the situation. You must be firm in voice and mannerisms. The client wants to lean on you—not vice versa.

Give the Client Directions

Tell the client "Follow me, please" to direct the client from the reception room to your office. When you get to your office door (which you should have left open when you went to the reception room), stop at the door and say, "This is my office" (especially if there is more than one room which could be your office). "Please go in."

Tell the Client Where to Sit

Tell the client, "Please, sit down,"indicating with a hand gesture the chair you wish the client to occupy. Help the client, if the client is injured or elderly. Ask the client if he or she is comfortable.

Close the Door and Sit Down Yourself

Insure Privacy

Call your secretary or the receptionist to tell her, "I'm in conference with Ms. Smith. No calls, please." Tell the client that when you're in conference you don't take calls, except for emergencies, because the client who is in your office is entitled to all your attention, and because you don't like to discuss one client's legal matters in front of another client.

Start Your Interview

Actually, the client started the interview with you when you came into the reception room. Now you are starting your interview of the client.

Ask Simple Questions

Start with simple questions such as name, home address, mailing address, home telephone, work telephone, etc. Establish the format immediately whereby you will ask the questions and the client will answer them.

Keep Control of the Situation

If the client is verbose and will not stop talking, tell the client that he or she must learn to answer questions and not to answer more than the question asked. Tell the client that each question and answer may have legal significance and that the client must listen carefully to the question and answer it carefully.

Make Tissues, Candy and an Ash Tray Available

If the client cries, offer tissues and ask if he or she would like a drink of water. Ask the client if he or she would rather finish the interview another time. (The client never says yes, but appreciates the offer.) Cigarettes may annoy you, but remember that tobacco is an addiction and it is easy to moralize about other people's addictions. Remember that the client may have a physical craving for the cigarette and he or she is paying you—not vice versa. Open a window if you have to, but don't ask the client not to smoke. On the other hand, you shouldn't smoke without first asking the client's permission.

Limit Your Interview to Between One and One and a Half Hours

Interviews longer than this are physically and mentally exhausting and should be avoided if possible.

Discuss Fees at the End of the Interview

If the client tries to bring up fees at the beginning of the interview or before the end of the interview, tell the client that you don't want to discuss fees until you've gotten all the facts and have a better idea of what's involved. Tell the client that your first concern is to hear the facts, so you can tell the client what kind of help is needed. At the end of the interview, discuss the fees and then dictate the fee engagement letter in the presence of the client.

Always Ask the Client What He or She Wants to Add

Tell the client that sometimes in the interviewing process facts get overlooked. Say to the client, "Is there anything you want to tell me or ask me?" If you've done a good job with the interview there won't be anything else. You'd be surprised at some of the things clients ask you or want to tell you.

End the Interview

The client is dependent on you to say when the interview is over. The easiest way to end the interview is simply to stand up and walk over to the door. Tell the client when you want to see or talk to him or her again, or say that you'll begin work as soon as the fee engagement letter with the retainer fee is returned.

Walk the Client Back to the Reception Room

Don't assume the client knows the way out. Shake hands with the client and say you are happy to have met him or her and look forward to working on the case.

How to Maintain Bank Accounts

The day you open your office, you should open three checking accounts, as follows:

Personal Account

The checks, check book and deposit slips should be printed "Personal Account." Use this account for nonoffice-related matters, such as food, clothing, etc. Your spouse may be a signator on the account to write checks if you desire.

Office Account

The checks, check book and deposit slips should be printed "Office Account." This account should be used for all items which are, or which might be, related to the practice income and expenses. Your spouse or your secretary can sign on this account.

Trust Account

The checks, check book and deposit slips should be printed "Trust Account." This account is for *client money*. You should *never* use it for your money. No person other than you should be able to sign on this account. You should *not* allow your spouse or a secretary or even another attorney to sign on this account. In some states the rules of trust account maintenance are set by the state bar in order to get the interest income. A more detailed discussion of the Trust Account will follow later.

Other Accounts

1. *Savings Accounts.* It is rare that you would have any use for a savings account insofar as your practice is concerned. Any interest income on trust accounts would belong to the client, not to you. (In some countries the attorney can keep the interest, but not in the U.S.) It is possible that where you will keep a large sum of client money for a significant time, that an interest-bearing account in your name, as trustee for the client, should be used, but this is an exceptional situation, and generally you should not keep trust account funds in an interest-bearing account.

2. *Payroll Account.* I recommend maintaining a separate checking account for payroll and payroll taxes, even though it is not required. As a practicing CPA, I learned to have a healthy respect for payroll taxes. When I hired my first secretary, I immediately opened a payroll account, and used the special payroll checks with appropriate spaces on the check and the stub to indicate the computation of the net pay. In some states, an employee is entitled by law to a statement of computation of the net pay, and the check with the computation will usually satisfy that requirement.

I also recommend transferring to the payroll account from the office account an amount equal to the *gross pay,* plus a flat percent allowance (10% to 12% is usually sufficient) to cover the employer share of the various payroll taxes, and worker's compensation, etc. In this manner, you set aside all payroll money as you go along, and don't have to worry about coming up with the payroll taxes monthly or quarterly.

It is foolish, in my opinion, to attempt to use or spend the difference between the employees' gross pay and the employees' net pay. This practice has led to serious problems for employers when they couldn't come up with the taxes withheld.

For example, assume a secretary is entitled to $100.00 gross pay, and the employer taxes are 6 percent Social Security, 1 percent Worker's Compensation, 3 percent Unemployment Insurance; assume 1 percent State Disability, and another 1 percent State Withholding and 20 percent Federal Withholding:

Gross Pay	$100.00
Employer Taxes:	
Social Security	$6.00
Worker's Compensation	1.00
Unemployment	3.00
	10.00

Amount to be transferred from Office account to Payroll Account:		$110.00
Gross Pay		$100.00
Less Deduction:		
State Disability	$ 1.00	
State Withholding	1.00	
Federal Withholding	20.00	
Total Deductions:		22.00
Net to Secretary:		$ 78.00

It is very tempting to only set aside $78.00 and to hope to have the balance of $42.00 when the time comes to pay the taxes. It will give you great peace of mind to set aside the entire payroll cost at the time of paying the payroll, and then not have to be concerned about coming up with the balance.

Failure to make withholding deposits can be criminal.

"Laundering Money"

Be very careful when a client or prospective client asks you to deposit a check or cash to one of your accounts in exchange for one of your checks; or when you purchase a cashier's check for the client often payable to a third party. Banks shouldn't practice law, and lawyers shouldn't engage in banking. There is sometimes a valid reason for your handling a "secret" transaction for a client (such as sealed bids); however, be careful.

Picking a Bank or Banker

As a new attorney in practice, some banks or bankers will go out of their way to accommodate you. Others will not want your business until you are more firmly established. Normally the reason a bank wants your business is to get your trust account deposits. You may have anywhere from a few hundred dollars to hundreds of thousands in your trust account for days, weeks or months. Since your checking account doesn't draw interest, the bank will want these deposits. This may be modified by statute in those states where the state bar wants the interest income. Start with the bank or branch closest to your office (for convenience), and tell the manager that you are starting your practice and want to establish a banking relationship. Do the same thing with two or three banks. See which bank or banker seems more interested in you, and open your accounts with that bank or banker. A good relationship will give you access to loan funds as you need them for temporary cash flow problems, as well as equipment financing and other personal banking needs.

What to expect from the bank you select:

1. No service charges on any of your accounts.
2. Free check printing (within limits).
3. Lunch with the banker, at bank expense.
4. Wills and trusts form books.
5. Favored treatment on your banking needs.

Getting Business from Banks and Bankers

Banks and bankers are an excellent source of business for a lawyer. They are frequently asked to recommend a lawyer to a customer.

Unfortunately, the new lawyer will rarely get any of these referrals, which usually will go to the bank's general counsel, or to lawyers who give the bank a lot of business. The bank's general counsel is often represented on the board or key committees of the bank. A branch manager may not wish to place his or her own position at risk by referring business to lawyers.

Occasionally, a bank customer will specifically ask the bank manager to recommend a new lawyer, or a young lawyer, to handle a case that other lawyers have already declined to handle.

Look upon these referrals as a golden opportunity to demonstrate how hard you can work. Don't make unrealistic promises to the client. Be honest as to the merit or lack of merit of the case. If you handle it, work as hard as you can. The banker may learn of the customer's satisfaction from the customer, and you may get a referral on a good client or matter.

How to Maintain a Trust Account to Avoid Disbarment

When I read the disciplinary reports which say "and shall be disbarred effective January 1, 19____, and his/her name shall forever be removed from the roll of attorneys of the state," a chill goes through me. I think of the years of study gone to waste; I think of the shame and tears of parents, the dashed hopes of the spouse; the fears of wondering how to provide for children and of having to explain to the children years later about their disbarred parent. I think of the high degree of suicide among disbarred lawyers. Most of all, I think about the client or clients who may have gone under with the unfortunate lawyer.

There are many ways to get yourself disbarred. The surest, fastest way to lose your license is to ignore the rules for handling client funds.

If you are going to get involved with "close practices" with client funds, remember that in this game every rule in the book is written against you. The referees (your state disciplinary board) will not look for extenuating circumstances, and ignorance on your part is no defense.

If you ignore this section of my book, you are not only a fool, you are a damned fool. I cannot emphasize strongly enough the importance to you of understanding and applying the rules of Trust Funds.

Many attorneys are disciplined for various matters, ranging from failure to return telephone calls to fee disputes. Attorneys are sometimes thrown out of bar associations for violating ethical rules. However, most disbarments result from mishandling of client funds.

You can still practice law after being kicked out of the local bar associations. You can still practice law after your period of discipline is over. You can never, never practice law again if you are disbarred.

With this background in mind, let's examine the basic rule and some practical examples of how to apply it in your everyday situations.

Disciplinary Rule 9-102 is a carry-forward of ABA Canon 11 and will be found in the law of your state, either as part of the Rules of Court or codified in your Business and Professional Code or in your general laws. I recommend highly that you read the exact wording of the law in your state as well as some of the annotations to get a sense of how easy it is to get disbarred.

The basic rules are as follows:

"DR 9-102 Preserving Identity of Funds and Property of a Client.
   (A) All funds of clients paid to a lawyer or law firm, other than advances for costs and expenses, shall be deposited in one or more identifiable bank accounts maintained in the state in which the law office is situated and no funds belonging to the lawyer or law firm shall be deposited therein except as follows:
       (1) Funds reasonably sufficient to pay bank charges may be deposited therein.
       (2) Funds belonging in part to a client and in part presently or potentially to the lawyer or law firm must be deposited therein, but the portion belonging to the lawyer or law firm may be withdrawn when due unless the right of the lawyer or law firm to receive it is disputed by the client, in which event the disputed portion shall not be withdrawn until the dispute is finally resolved.
   (B) A lawyer shall:
       (1) Promptly notify a client of the receipt of his funds, securities, or other properties.
       (2) Identify and label securities and properities of a client promptly upon receipt and place them in a safe deposit box or other place of safekeeping as soon as practicable.
       (3) Maintain complete records of all funds, securities, and other properties of a client coming into the possession of the lawyer and render appropriate acounts to his client regarding them.
       (4) Promptly pay or deliver to the client as requested by a client the funds, securities, or other properties in the posssession of the lawyer which the client is entitled to receive."

Opening a Trust Checking Account

1. Title the account "Trust Account" or a similar wording. Although the word "Trust" is not required *per se,* I recommend it.

2. Use a red checkbook cover. The color red obviously indicates "Danger."

3. Use checks of a color different from your office or payroll checks.

4. Yours should be the only authorized signature. Do not allow your spouse, secretary or office manager to sign the checks.

5. Reconcile the account monthly.

Don't use savings accounts unless there are very exceptional circumstances. I am continually confronted by new lawyers who get the bright idea of putting trust funds into savings accounts to get interest on the "float." I have to deflate the egos of these financial wizards by pointing out two basic fallacies in the scheme:

1. The funds are the clients' and the interest on the clients' funds belongs to the clients whose money earned the interest.

2. DR 9-102(B)(1) requires the funds to be *promptly* paid to the client. Delaying the payment to the client in order to earn interest is not proper in any event, in my opinion, even if you did send the interest to the client.

I have been told, but have not independently verified, that attorneys in some countries can ethically and legally keep the interest earned on client funds. This may explain in part the delay I have experienced in getting client money from overseas lawyers.

In any event, if you have several clients' money in a savings account, you would have to bookkeep on a daily basis which client had earned the interest. The amount of work involved for the amount of interest involved for a particular client usually will not justify your going through all the work of computing the interest.

Don't pay personal bills from the account. If you have a fee in the trust account which you are entitled to, don't just spend the money from the trust account. Transfer the fee from the trust account to the office account, then transfer your draw from the office account to your personal account. Thus, you will have a clean record, and no explanations will be necessary at a later time.

Don't make any disbursements without a client's written authorization. Ordinarily, your fee agreement contains your written authorization to reimburse yourself any costs and fees you're entitled to.

Suppose client Jim Jones whom you are representing on a good accident case has an unrelated problem such as a criminal or domestic relations matter. He wants you to work on the unrelated case with you getting your fee from his share of the proceeds of the accident case.

1. *Can you ethically do this?* Yes. A client may engage you on an unrelated matter and you may agree to defer the time of payment until the accident case closes.

2. *Can you take the money from the trust account when the case closes?* Yes, providing you have the authorization to pay the fees in writing. You must understand that when you have client funds in your trust account, you are a fiduciary. When the client owes you a fee, you are a creditor. You must act as a fiduciary with the trust fund, even though your client acts as a debtor with the unpaid fee.

3. *Suppose your client disputes part of your fee; can you take the undisputed portion out of the trust account?* Yes. You *must* withdraw from the trust account your funds and you *must* forward to the client his or her funds.

Suppose your client engages you and gives you a retainer check of $725, representing a $250 minimum fee, $350 towards additional fees (if your fee exceeds $250) and $125 in costs. What do you do?

1. Deposit the check to your trust account.

2. Wait three to five banking days for the check to clear (unless you want to take a chance on your client's credit).

3. Withdraw your $250 minimum fee immediately because it is yours in any event and must be withdrawn (unless your fee agreement specifies otherwise).

4. Pay for costs out of the trust account as incurred. Stop when costs reach $125. At this point, either get more money from your client or advance costs from your office account. Do not use the "excess" fee funds. You may be obligated to return them if not used.

5. When you and the client have agreed in writing to your "excess fee," you may withdraw it from the trust account.

Suppose client Jane Jones owes you $125 for a loan or for fees or costs on an unrelated matter. You then settle a case for her and have $35,000 in your trust account which belongs to her.

1. *Can you simply send her a check for $34,875?* No. Again, you are a fiduciary with respect to the $35,000 and a creditor with respect to the $125. Therefore, you must send her the $35,000 and ask for your $125.

2. *Is there some way you can withhold the $125 from the trust*

funds? Yes. Simply get her permission in writing to pay yourself the $125 from her trust funds.

How do you get clients to agree in writing to your taking the fees from the trust funds? The simplest way is to send a letter explaining what you wish to do and ask him or her to sign the carbon copy indicating permission and to send the signed copy back to you by mail. If you simply stick a piece of paper in front of the client and tell him or her to sign it, there may be a later claim that the letter wasn't understood when it was signed. By getting the letter mailed back to you, the client presumably had time to consider what was being agreed to.

Is it required that the permission be given in writing? There is nothing in the Code which requires the permission to be in writing. However, you will be in a difficult situation two or three years later when the client simultaneously sues you, alleging a breach of fiduciary duty, and files a complaint with the state bar for unauthorized use of trust funds. Clients (and some lawyers) have a tendency to remember only what they want to remember, and it will be a matter of your word versus the client's word.

Insurance Needs
of the New Lawyer

Insurance is an expense which new lawyers hate to pay since there is a cash disbursement with no probability of profit. However painful it might be, accept the fact that you are a complete and total fool if you are not adequately insured.

Malpractice Insurance

Accept two basic facts:

1. You are responsible for malpractice, even if you did someone "a favor," and did not charge or collect a fee;

2. At some time during your career, you wil be sued for malpractice.

Whether you want to call it "errors and omissions" or "malpractice" or "professional negligence," it is the insurance that protects you, your clients and third parties when you get sued. Often the costs of defense alone will be many, many times what you paid in premiums.

As a general rule, your local bar association will have gotten the best "deal" available for you. Sometimes a private agent or broker can get you a better "deal." Be careful. From time to time, insurance companies simply go out of the malpractice insurance business, and you may find yourself stranded without coverage. As a member of your local bar association, you will be part of a larger economic unit in a better bargaining position.

There is no substitute for working with a good insurance agent or broker who has your interests at heart. The purpose of this section is not to replace the broker, but rather to educate both you and the broker in the peculiarities of insurance as it affects a new lawyer in practice. Keep in mind that the terminology for insurance coverage changes from time to time and from place to place.

There are some points you should be careful about.

1. *"Gaps" in Coverage.* Some policies are "claims" policies and some are "occurrence" policies. The difference can best be illustrated by a hypothetical example. Suppose Company "A" insured you for 1984 on a "claim" basis, and Company "B" insures you on an "occurrence" basis in 1985. Suppose you commit a negligent act in 1984, and a claim is made against you in 1985. Company "A" will not cover you because the "claim" wasn't made during the policy period 1984, and Company "B" will not cover you because the "occurrence" didn't occur during its policy period, 1985. Therefore, even though you had policies in effect at all times, you have no coverage.

Another important thing to remember is that any time you change carriers, be sure that you don't have any gaps in your coverage.

2. *Settlement Approval.* If possible, try to get a policy that gives you the right to approve settlements being made. The problem here is to avoid the stigma or rating problem in the future when a settlement is made of a nonmeritorious claim.

3. *Deductible.* Many policies now provide for significant deductibility of $1,000 or more, *including costs of defense.* In other words, you must pay the first $1,000 of defense costs incurred.

4. *Exclusions.* There is a tendency for insurance companies to reduce risk by excluding certain areas of practice from coverage, such as securities. Be sure you read and understand your policy.

5. *Sufficient coverage.* From time to time, you may have a very significant case matter, involving large amounts of money, and large exposure if you are negligent. Give consideration to buying more insurance to cover that matter, and don't be afraid to raise your fee so that you are adequately compensated, giving effect to the cost of the premium. Remember that insurance protects both you *and* your client.

Umbrella Coverage

"Umbrella" or excess coverage, in my opinion, is the best insurance value available, considering premium cost and coverage. Oversimplified, it picks up coverage where your underlying policies do not. For example, it normally would be cheaper for you to have a $300,000 malpractice policy and a $1,000,000 umbrella (in effect, a $1,300,000 policy with a $300,000 deductible), than to have a $1,000,000 malpractice policy. Additionally, the umbrella will often pick up the "excess" coverage in other areas of insurance besides malpractice. Any time your broker or agent quotes you rates for malpractice or other liability insurance, ask for quotes on rates for the same coverage using a smaller "underlying policy" with an umbrella coverage.

Nonowned Autos

Be sure you and your office help are covered if there is an auto accident when an employee is running an errand for you, such as going to the post office to mail that rush, rush letter.

Office Furniture, Etc.

Be sure that you are insured for "replacement value." In our inflationary times, insurance which pays claims based on cost less depreciation is close to having no insurance at all. Don't assume that just because the insurance company takes your premium based on present-day replacement costs that they will pay claims based on present-day replacement cost. Here again, either read your policy or get a good broker.

File Replacement and Cost of Insurance for Valuable Papers

For the first year or two, you will not have much concern over this problem, but ultimately, this type of coverage will be extremely important to you. This coverage includes the cost of replacing your files, rather than the value of the paper in the files. In the event of fire, it could cost you thousands of dollars to buy photocopies of documents, letters, etc., from the courts and clients and other attorneys to reconstruct your files.

Workers' Compensation

Remember to get this coverage when you hire your first secretary. That person may be real clumsy and push a typewriter off the desk onto a foot the first day of employment. Your first secretary's first task should be to call your broker to be sure of insurance coverage. If your state has a state fund or state policy, you should check their rates during your first year or two of coverage. With only one secretary or clerk you may fall within the "minimum premium" cost category.

The minimum is often substantially lower with state-owned companies or funds than privately owned companies.

Office Block Insurance

This is a "package" available in some areas which combines several types of insurance which a law office needs into a single "block" or package. It is similar to the concept of "homeowners" package insurance. Here again, you need the help of a good broker.

Other Types of Insurance

The other types of insurance are not peculiar to new lawyers in practice and will be simply listed as a check list here.

1. *Disability Insurance or Office Overhead Insurance.* Buy all you can afford. In my opinion, this type of insurance is more necessary than life insurance. Life insurance protects *others* if you die. Disability insurance protects *you* if you live. If you get sick or disabled and can't work, both your office overhead and your home overhead will continue. In some states, you are eligible for state coverage.

It is my opinion that, as a general rule, you should purchase this insurance through your bar association during your early years. It is not unknown for some insurance companies in this area to be very eager to accept premiums for coverage and later threaten you with cancellation and refusal to pay.

Unfortunately, when you need this coverage you need it badly and cannot afford the luxury of collecting your money with 7 percent interest three years later when you win your lawsuit against the insurance company. Possibly you will not be able to wait even the three to six months involved for the insurance company doctor to examine you and send a report to the insurance company. As part of the larger bar group, you and your claim will be in a better position to get faster payment of just claims. Insurance companies have been known to act rapidly when faced with the loss of hundreds or thousands of policies. On the other hand, if the insurance company drops the entire bar association (or vice versa), you'll have lost the bargaining position and might have been better off with your own broker.

Given all factors, I repeat my recommendation that you buy this coverage through your bar association for the first few years of your practice.

2. *Life Insurance.* Don't be pressured by arguments of how cheaply you can buy a six-figure policy "at your age." Remember that in your early years, cash flow and conservation are your biggest problems. Although premiums will be higher five years later, you'll be in a better position to pay for the higher coverage when you have the income. I suggest you investigate one-year renewable term insurance with your broker.

3. *Public Liability, Fire, Employee Bonding, ERISA, Health, Comprehensive, Medical, Notary Bond, etc.* These are general insurance problems not peculiar to new lawyers in practice and a competent broker or agent should be able to help you.

Checklist on Insurance Coverage

Contact or obtain an insurance broker or agent who is likely to refer you business (old family broker, if possible), or buy from different brokers:

1. Malpractice Insurance (Errors & Omissions). Get occurrence rather than claims-made coverage, if possible.

2. General Liability Insurance for Office.

3. Workers' Compensation.

4. Non-owned automobile insurance.

5. File replacement and valuable papers coverage.

6. Fire and Theft (get replacement value).

7. Get "Umbrella" coverage, if available.

8. Check with broker or bank for "premium financing" (monthly payments).

9. Check if "Office Block" policy is available.

Why You Need
a Personnel Manual

As strange as it may seem, you should have a personnel manual *before* you hire your first employee. As a general rule, lawyers are soft-hearted and don't like to do unpleasant tasks, such as docking or firing employees who are habitually sick or late, or who abuse common rules of good office systems and decorum. Additionally, you, as a new lawyer, have had little or no experience or ability in personnel management. If you doubt this, figure out how you would handle the following factual situations:

1. For the third time in two weeks your clerk Jack calls in at 10:05 to say he's late because of car trouble.

2. Your 45-year-old secretary comes to work in Levis, T-shirt and no bra and torn tennis shoes. She calls you a male chauvinist pig for asking her to dress more conventionally and says she'll file a civil rights suit against you based on sex discrimination if you fire her or discipline her.

3. Your secretary is "into" Zen Buddhism and claims the right to a paid holiday for Buddha's birthday, equating it to Christmas for Christians and Rosh Hashana for Jews. Again, the threat of a civil rights suit.

4. Cigarette smoke annoys you, and your secretary insists on smoking on the job (or vice versa).

5. Your secretary takes home expensive legal pads for a spouse's night-school note-taking.

6. Your secretary claims time and one-half for dropping the mail into a mailbox on the way home.

7. After two months on the job, your clerk tells you a grandmother died, and he has to take one month off, and expects his job to be waiting for him.

Believe it or not, the above factual situations, and some even more bizarre, have happened to me over a period of years. It is not satisfactory to wait for problems to occur and then try to handle them on an *ad hoc* basis. You should have an employee office manual ready for *your first* employee. As a final step in the hiring process, you should hand the manual to the employee, getting a signed receipt in which it is acknowledged that it was read and understood and the employee agrees to be bound by it. Such things as tardiness, absences, sickness, holidays, overtime, dress, office supplies, etc., would ordinarily be covered in the office personnel manual.

Given that you now understand the need for a manual, where do you get one?

1. Create your own manual. The Fall 1975 issue of *Legal Economics,* published by the Section on Economics of Law Practice of the ABA, 1155 East 60th Street, Chicago, IL 60637, contains an excellent check list for a complete manual. The issue is out of print, but you can get copies of the check list and the bibliography entitled "Where to Go for Help" referred to in my chapter of the same name.

2. Copy another lawyer's personnel manual. This is one of those rare situations where a poor or mediocre solution is better than none. Use the other lawyer's manual until you can modify it for your particular purposes.

Subjects for Office Personnel Policy

Following is an alphabetical list of elements that should be considered for inclusion in an office personnel policy:

Absences	Funeral pay	Noise	Soliciting of employees
Accidents	Garnishments	Office supplies	Suggestions
Attitude	Gossip	Overtime	Supervisors
Bonding of employees	Grievances	Parking	Tardiness
Bulletin boards	Health insurance	Pay day	Telephone courtesy
Cleanliness	Holidays	Pay period	Temporary employment
Clothing	Housekeeping	Pension plan	Terminal vacation
Coffee breaks	Intoxication	Personal phone calls	Termination of employment
Complaints	Introduction	Personal mail	Time cards
Confidential nature of work	Jury duty	Personal visitors	Trial period
Contracts	Labor laws	Personnel counseling	Unemployment insurance
Decorum	Leaves of absence	Privileged communications	Vacations
Deductions	Liability & malpractice	Privileged info	Work evaluations
Disability insurance	insurance	Probationary period	Work habits
Discounts	Loyalty	Professional ethics	Work periods
Discrimination	Lunches	Promotions	Working hours
Dismissal	Magazines	Re-employment	Workers' compensation
Dress	Marriage & pregnancy	Resignations	
Economy	Maternity	Retirement	
Emergencies	Meal schedules	Safety	
Emergency leave	Medical care	Salary	
Employee addresses	Meetings	Salary calculation	
Employee lounge	Merit review	Salary increases	
Employee personality	Military service	Schedules	
Employee-client relations	Misconduct	Sick leave	
Employee roster	Moonlighting	Smoking	
Fire	New employees	Social security	

Bookkeeping and Accounting Systems

Get a CPA.

Unless you have some accounting knowledge or bookkeeping experience, you really shouldn't try to maintain your own books or prepare your own income tax return. I am a Board Certified Specialist in Taxation and I am a Certified Public Accountant, but I don't maintain my own books or prepare my own tax returns. I am simply applying the old maxim, "The lawyer who represents himself has a fool for a client."

1. A CPA can be an excellent source of clients for a lawyer. CPAs normally are in periodic close contact with their clients. These clients frequently ask the CPA to recommend a lawyer for the problems of the business, and the employees of the business.

2. Try to select a CPA in a small- or medium-size CPA firm. A large firm rarely can refer anything to a new lawyer and may not have the same interest in you as a client as a small- or medium-size firm.

3. Unfortunately, you probably won't be able to send much business to the CPA. CPAs send many more clients to lawyers than vice versa. As a new lawyer, the kind of work you can generate for a CPA (other than your own accounting) is call "special engagement" work, such as looking for assets in marital cases.

In any event you need some simple accounting procedures and systems for your day-to-day financial transactions.

Keep It Simple

You won't have many transactions your first year or two, so you really don't need a national CPA firm with an IBM 370 Computer.

A simple checkbook for your office expense checks should be adequate. If you want to use a four-part snapout checkbook for client costs, you can.

Your accountant will probably recommend a "write-it-once" system for you.

Read the chapter on bank accounts and the simplified "chart of accounts" which follows this chapter. Note that the trust account does not appear on your statements since the money in that account is not yours. Your accountant may wish to show the account with a *"contra"* or offset. This is an area of theoretical debate among accountants. The important thing is that you do not include the trust account on your financial statements.

Leave Tracks

An accountant can easily reconstruct transactions if you leave tracks. Put explanations on your duplicate bank deposit slips and explain in detail what you are writing checks for.

Use Cash Basis Books

For income tax purposes you'll want to be on the cash basis. After you're in practice a few years you can get sophisticated with accounts receivable and accruals, but not at the beginning.

Buy the ABA Monographs

The American Bar Association Economics of Law Practice Section (750 N. Lake Shore Drive, Chicago, Illinois 60611) publishes several monographs on law office accounting. You should buy one of each that is available and keep it as part of your permanent library for your CPA to use. Let your CPA firm buy their own set. Don't let them remove yours from your office. I contributed to several of the monographs in various capacities and recommend them highly.

Chart of Accounts for the New Lawyer

Assets
Cash in Bank—Office
Cash in Bank—Payroll
Client Costs Receivable
Deposits—Lease, Utilities, etc.
Deposit Account—Sheriff and
  Marshal
Prepaid Expenses
Desks and Chairs (accumulated
  depreciation)
Typewriters (accumulated
  depreciation)
Dictating Equipment (ac-
  cumulated depreciation)
Other Office Equipment (ac-
  cumulated depreciation)
Library (accumulated
  depreciation)
Lease Hold Improvements (ac-
  cumulated depreciation)

Liabilities
Withheld Payroll Taxes Payable
Equipment Contracts Payable
Bank Loans Payable
Other Liabilities

Capital
John Lawyer Capital
John Lawyer Draw
  (Nondeductible)
John Lawyer Draw (Deductible)

Income
Fees Received—
  Personal Injury
  Domestic Relations
  Criminal
  Business
  Probate
  Other

Expenses
Accounting
Associate Fees
Attorney Service
Auto
Bank Charges
Business Promotion
Continuing Education
Depreciation
Dues, Professional
Employee Meals and Incentives
Employee Procurement
Equipment Rental
Insurance
Interest
Investigation, Investigators (non-
  receivable)
Medical Insurance
Meetings and Seminars
Office Supplies
Outside Secretarial
Payroll Taxes
Postage
Postage Equipment Rental
Professional Periodicals
Rent—Office
Rent—Parking
Repairs and Maintenance
Salaries—Secretaries
Salaries—Office
Salaries—Clerks
Stationery and Printing
Taxes and Licenses
Telephone
Travel and Conventions
Photocopier Rental and Supplies

Simple Filing Systems
for the New Lawyer

File Cabinets

If a well-meaning relative bought you an old-fashioned two- or four-drawer file cabinet, throw it out or give it to charity; but don't use it. Use vertical files. (See sample on exhibit following this chapter.)

Using vertical files, you can store two and a half times as many files in the same space or, to put it another way, your rental cost for floor space when using vertical files is 25 percent that when using horizontal files.

A file cabinet will usually occupy about six square feet (including drawer pull-out space). At 50 cents per month per square foot (a nominal rent), you'll pay $3.00 per month or $36.00 per year for that file cabinet. The cost per file is four times the cost of using vertical files. Use low-cost shelving instead.

Ask your stationery store for samples of each type.

Organizing the File

Keep it simple. There are dozens of systems for organizing files. Some are good for personal injury plaintiff, some are good for personal injury defendant, some are good for probate, some are good for wills and estate planning. Some systems appear to have been invented by geniuses, some appear to have been invented by idiots. My advice to the new lawyer is to ignore all these fancy file folder systems until you are somewhat established and can appreciate and understand what you actually need in a filing system. I suggest a simple file folder as illustrated in the exhibit at the end of this chapter.

Keep everything in chronological order. Don't open multiple files for the same matter. After a couple of years, this system will probably become inadequate for you. At that time you can make changes depending upon your specific needs.

Use a Numerical Filing System

The simplest and best system for you is to use a year-matter system. Each year start a new series. For example, 83-1, 83-2, 83-3, etc., then 84-1, 84-2, 84-3, etc. If you are embarrassed over the small number of files you have, then cheat on the numbering system. About February 1 of each year simply add 200 or 300 to the last nunber so that in February your numbering system would start with 83-202, 83-203, etc. Other lawyers will think you're doing a lot of business.

Make an alphabetical cross-index system, putting the client names on index cards cross-referenced to the file number.

When and How to Open and Close Files

1. *Opening files.* Open a file when you have a client and a case and are professionally responsible for the matter. Until then, keep the copies of the documents, letters, etc., in 26 alphabetical, miscellaneous files, each in chronological order. When you open the file, remove the documents from the miscellaneous file and put them in the separate numerical file for the client matter. If you never open a file, simply leave the documents in the miscellaneous file for that alphabetical letter.

2. *Open a new file for each matter.* Believe me, it will make your life much easier to keep each matter in a totally different file with its own file number.

3. *Closing files.* After you've been in practice a few years you can get involved with microfilming. Until then, stick with my simple system.

a. Fill out a closed file sheet. It will replace the bulky file and become the basis of future work. This closed file sheet can be kept in a three-ring notebook in your office. The filling out of this form will serve as a "last chance" to clean up any loose ends or errors you spot. A sample closed file information sheet follows this chapter.

b. Remove duplicate copies of documents that you know will never be needed. (Remember pleadings can always be obtained from the court.)

c. Send valuable original documents back to the client with a cover letter (unless you enjoy being a bailee-insurer of the item).

d. Get the file folder out of your high-rent office to a low-rent or no-rent storage area and file it in numerical order.

e. Remove the alpha-numeric cross-index card from the active index and put it in the closed file card index.

4. *When to close a file.* Close the file when there is nothing more for you to do on the case and when you've informed the client in writing that you are doing nothing further and are closing your file.

5. *When to destroy a file.* I'm a coward and have never destroyed files. Other more courageous lawyers than I close them after three-year or five-year intervals. I don't recommend file destruction. Microfilm them before destruction.

Color Filing to Prevent Lost and Misplaced Files

During your first year or two, lost or misplaced or misfiled files will not be a problem. As time goes on and you accumulate a large number of folders, misplaced files can be a serious problem. I invented a color filing system which virtually eliminates misfiled files. Simply get your file folders in different colors. When I last counted, 13 different colors were commercially available. *Change colors* every 100 files or every letter. For example, all file folders for matters 83-1 through 83-99 are blue; from 83-100 through 83-199 red; from 83-200 through 83-299 green; from 84-1 through 84-99 orange, etc. Or use "A's," "B's," "C's," etc., and have a different color folder.

The theory is simple. You can misfile a red folder in the section with the other red folders, but you can't misfile it in the green folder section or the brown folder section. Believe me, the system works.

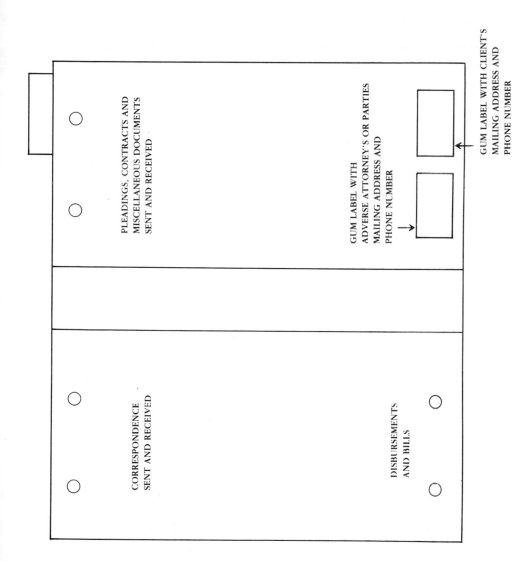

PLEADINGS, CONTRACTS AND
MISCELLANEOUS DOCUMENTS
SENT AND RECEIVED

GUM LABEL WITH
ADVERSE ATTORNEY'S OR PARTIES
MAILING ADDRESS AND
PHONE NUMBER

GUM LABEL WITH CLIENT'S
MAILING ADDRESS AND
PHONE NUMBER

CORRESPONDENCE
SENT AND RECEIVED

DISBURSEMENTS
AND BILLS

Closed File Sheet

Closed File No._____   Original File No._____

INFORMATION FOR CLOSED FILES

Court Case No._____

1. Title of case as it appears on file_____
2. Nature or type of case_____
3. Names of our clients _____
4. Last known business and residence addresses and phone numbers of our clients _____
5. Date file closed _____
6. Reason file closed _____
7. Who authorized closing of file? _____
8. Letter in file advising client file has been closed?
   Yes_____ No_____
9. Letter in file advising client we will do nothing further?
   Yes_____ No_____ If so, date of letter_____
10. Any Statutues of Limitations involved? Yes_____ No_____
    If so, is Statue of Limitations indicated in either of above
    letters? Yes_____ No_____
11. Any original documents of client in file? Yes_____
    No_____ If so, specify _____
    _____
12. At time of closing file, any unpaid fees or costs due?
    Yes_____ No_____ If so, amount: $ _____
13. List all plaintiffs in case_____
    _____
14. List of all defendants in case _____
    _____
15. Description of last document or pleading in file (include
    date) _____
16. Date and nature of last contact (letter, call, meeting, etc.)
    _____
17. Number of file folders and estimated thickness in inches
    No._____ Thickness_____
18. Is party a minor? Yes_____ No_____ If yes, date of birth
    and indicated activity required upon majority _____
    _____
    Has client been advised as to what must be done upon majority? Yes_____ No_____

19. Dismissals filed? Yes_____ No_____ If yes, against whom?

_____

With prejudice_____ Without prejudice_____

20. Abstract of Judgment in file? Yes_____ No_____ If yes, recorded?_____ Date of recording _____ Released?_____ Date of release _____

21. Satisfaction of Judgment in file? Yes_____ No_____ If yes, recorded? _____ Date of recording _____ Amount of Satisfaction _____ If Partial Satisfaction, indicate amount, date, if recorded _____

22. Date judgment entered_____

23. What is there to do in the future?
    A. Review judgment after 10 years _____
    B. Disburse money (to whom?) _____
    C. Need renewal or notice because of lease _____
    D. Need renewal or notice because of provision in contract
    E. Trust involved? _____ If so, need to notify client when trust terminates or other reason for notifying client? Yes_____ No_____

24. Anything requiring us to notify client in the future? Yes_____ No_____ If so, what? _____

_____

When? _____

25. Has there been a request made on the 20-year calendar? Yes_____ No_____ If so, nature of request _____

_____

How to Build
a Good Form File

Your form file will be one of your most valuable assets. During the first few years you'll be doing a lot of things for the first time. You'll be copying from form books, from other lawyers, and you'll be doing a lot of drafting of forms. If you are like most lawyers, you'll want to copy prior work whenever possible, changing the names and adding or subtracting a few paragraphs. This practice is to be commended, provided you know what you are doing. Blindly copying pages of "boiler plate" language that is neither intelligible nor applicable will eventually get you or your client into trouble. Remember that many forms appear in form books because the intent of the drafter was either upheld, defeated or left uncertain in litigation over the wording of the form.

Keep in mind that during your first few years, the work of other more experienced lawyers is likely to be somewhat better than yours. Therefore it makes good sense to take the work of another lawyer *as a starting point* and improve from there.

In the final analysis there are only two things you need for a good form file. These two things are: (1) Good Forms, and (2) A Good Index to the Forms.

Good Forms

The best way to get good forms is to start with form books. Keep a healthy respect for the copyright laws but don't forget the doctrine of "Fair Use" which allows you to copy most forms which are not copyrighted, and to a certain extent some that are copyrighted. Normally, form books and pleadings are copyable for your own use without difficulty.

Save and hard copy everything that you feel is or may be useful to you. Put it into a permanent form file. Get the forms bound by a commercial bookbinder with your name engraved in gold on the outside. *Don't* use loose-leaf files, as over a period of time the best forms tend to disappear as you remove them and forget to replace them. The theory underscoring saving *everything* is that the latest form on a subject should be the best and you can put several together to develop what you need.

A Good Index to the Forms

You can either invent your own subject matter index starting from scratch, which is a gross waste of time, or you can use a system developed by experts at a cost of millions of dollars. The West Key Number System is a good one. A copy of the basic index form follows this chapter.

If your state has another index system which you feel is superior, then use it, but don't try to create your own (subject to a penchant for masochism on your part).

I recommend that you index everything that goes into your form file along the following classifications:

A. Subject matter (using the commercial index developed by someone else)

B. Client's name

C. Adverse party's name

D. Statutes involved

E. Court or tribunal in which you appeared

F. Judge or administrative person who heard the matter

G. Adverse attorney involved

You cannot over-index a document; you can only underindex it. Using this index system (which I invented and which you can copy), you'll be able to recall almost anything you've done or seen if it's in your form file. Admittedly, this form file will be of more value to you the longer you're in practice, but start it with the first document or pleading you prepare.

The above system will more than service your needs for the first few years of your practice. Eventually you should read *Retrieval Systems for Lawyers,* published by the Economics of Law Practice Section of the ABA (available at $22.00 – $12.00 to members of the

Section—from American Bar Association, Order Fulfillment 511, 750 N. Lake Shore Drive, Chicago, IL 60611).

You may also use forms prepared by opposing counsel, using OCR (optical character recognition) equipment to copy other lawyers' hard copy into your word-processing system.

WEST KEY NUMBERS AND TOPICS

1	Abandoned and Lost Property	
2	Abatement and Revival	
3	Abduction	
4	Abortion and Birth Control	
5	Absentees	
6	Abstracts of Title	
7	Accession	
8	Accord and Satisfaction	
9	Account	
10	Account, Action on	
11	Account Stated	
11A	Accountants	
12	Acknowledgment	
13	Action	
14	Action on the Case	
15	Adjoining Landowners	
15A	Administrative Law and Procedure	
16	Admiralty	
17	Adoption	
18	Adulteration	
19	Adultery	
20	Adverse Possession	
21	Affidavits	
22	Affray	
23	Agriculture	
24	Aliens	
25	Alteration of Instruments	
26	Ambassadors and Consuls	
27	Amicus Curiae	
28	Animals	
29	Annuities	
30	Appeal and Error	
31	Appearance	
33	Arbitration	
34	Armed Services	
35	Arrest	
36	Arson	
37	Assault and Battery	
38	Assignments	
40	Assistance, Writ of	
41	Associations	
42	Assumpsit, Action of	
43	Asylums	
44	Attachment	
45	Attorney and Client	
46	Attorney General	
47	Auctions and Auctioneers	
48	Audita Querela	
48A	Automobiles	
48B	Aviation	
49	Bail	
50	Bailment	
51	Bankruptcy	
52	Banks and Banking	
54	Beneficial Associations	
55	Bigamy	
56	Bills and Notes	
57	Blasphemy	
58	Bonds	
59	Boundaries	
60	Bounties	
61	Breach of Marriage Promise	
62	Breach of the Peace	
63	Bribery	
64	Bridges	
65	Brokers	
66	Building and Loan Associations	
67	Burglary	
68	Canals	
69	Cancellation of Instruments	
70	Carriers	
71	Cemeteries	
72	Census	
73	Certiorari	
74	Champerty and Maintenance	
75	Charities	
76	Chattel Mortgages	
76A	Chemical Dependents	
77	Citizens	
78	Civil Rights	
79	Clerks of Courts	
80	Clubs	
81	Colleges and Universities	
82	Collision	
83	Commerce	
84	Common Lands	
85	Common Law	
86	Common Scold	
88	Compounding Offenses	
89	Compromise and Settlement	
89A	Condominium	
90	Confusion of Goods	
91	Conspiracy	
92	Constitutional Law	
92B	Consumer Credit	
92H	Consumer Protection	
93	Contempt	
95	Contracts	
96	Contribution	
97	Conversion	
98	Convicts	
99	Copyrights and Intellectual Property	
100	Coroners	
101	Corporations	
102	Costs	
103	Counterfeiting	
104	Counties	
105	Court Commissioners	
106	Courts	
107	Covenant, Action of	
108	Covenants	
108A	Credit Reporting Agencies	
110	Criminal Law	
111	Crops	
113	Customs and Usages	
114	Customs Duties	
115	Damages	
116	Dead Bodies	
117	Death	
117G	Debt, Action of	
117T	Debtor and Creditor	
118A	Declaratory Judgment	
119	Dedication	
120	Deeds	
122A	Deposits and Escrows	
123	Deposits in Court	
124	Descent and Distribution	
125	Detectives	
126	Detinue	
129	Disorderly Conduct	
130	Disorderly House	
131	District and Prosecuting Attorneys	
132	District of Columbia	
133	Disturbance of Public Assemblage	
134	Divorce	
135	Domicile	
136	Dower and Curtesy	
137	Drains	
138	Drugs and Narcotics	
140	Dueling	
141	Easements	
142	Ejectment	
143	Election of Remedies	
144	Elections	
145	Electricity	
146	Embezzlement	
147	Embracery	
148	Eminent Domain	
148A	Employers' Liability	
149	Entry, Writ of	
150	Equity	
151	Escape	
152	Escheat	
154	Estates in Property	
156	Estoppel	
157	Evidence	
158	Exceptions, Bill of	
159	Exchange of Property	
160	Exchanges	
161	Execution	
162	Executors and Administrators	
163	Exemptions	
164	Explosives	
165	Extortion and Threats	
166	Extradition and Detainers	
167	Factors	
168	False Imprisonment	
169	False Personation	
170	False Pretenses	
170A	Federal Civil Procedure	
170B	Federal Courts	
171	Fences	
172	Ferries	
174	Fines	
175	Fires	
176	Fish	
177	Fixtures	
178	Food	
179	Forcible Entry and Detainer	
180	Forfeitures	
181	Forgery	
182	Fornication	
183	Franchises	
184	Fraud	
185	Frauds, Statute of	
186	Fraudulent Conveyances	
187	Game	
188	Gaming	
189	Garnishment	
190	Gas	
191	Gifts	
192	Good Will	
193	Grand Jury	
195	Guaranty	
196	Guardian and Ward	
197	Habeas Corpus	
198	Hawkers and Peddlers	
199	Health and Environment	
200	Highways	
201	Holidays	
202	Homestead	
203	Homicide	
204	Hospitals	
205	Husband and Wife	
205A	Illegitimate Children	
205H	Implied and Constructive Contracts	
206	Improvements	
207	Incest	
208	Indemnity	
209	Indians	
210	Indictment and Information	
211	Infants	
212	Injunction	
213	Innkeepers	
216	Inspection	
217	Insurance	
218	Insurrection and Sedition	
219	Interest	
220	Internal Revenue	
221	International Law	
222	Interpleader	
223	Intoxicating Liquors	

Beware of the Library Trap

I have devoted a large portion of this book to the subject of library because this is the single largest waste of money by new lawyers. For reasons that I don't understand, new lawyers rush out to buy books and periodicals that they don't need and can't afford.

Library expenses can be a bottomless pit. The gradual growth of your library and the corresponding increase in monthly payments can deprive you of cash when you need it most. Before ordering a book, put the order form in your desk drawer for 24 hours; then take it out and examine it again. Put it back in the desk drawer for another 24 hours and if you still feel you need the book, then sign the order form.

Free and Low-Cost Publications

These books are usually available from two sources: government and commercial.

Compose a form letter which you can have printed along the following lines:

Dear _____:

      I am a newly admitted lawyer about to open my own practice. I anticipate that I may have contact with your agency in the near future.

      I would appreciate being placed on your mailing list for publications and forms which you make available to attorneys. If there is a charge for the publication or forms either on a periodic or other basis, I would appreciate your informing me by return mail of the cost.

Thank you for your courtesy and cooperation.

Very truly yours,

J. Novice

Government Sources

Many government agencies distribute materials free or at nominal cost (less than a few dollars). Don't worry about getting or buying useless information. Any library contains some information that will never be used. The cost is so low that you can afford to make a few mistakes.

There is an element of surprise or grab bag involved. You'll be surprised to find which agencies administer which laws. In California the corporation checklist with invaluable information for forming corporations comes from the Secretary of State rather than the Department of Corporations. I got an adoption manual from the Department of Social Welfare for about $2.00. Within a few weeks I had my first adoption matter and every form and procedure was spelled out in detail. I also got a free subscription for all Security and Exchange Releases. After 20 years I'm still waiting for my first Security and Exchange case.

You should get the local phone books (from the phone company or public library) for your state capital, the largest commercial city in the state and your home town. Write to *every* agency listed under the state, county, city, and federal governments. If you are really ambitious you can get the Washington, D.C. phone book and write to every federal agency listed.

In the first few years get everything free and everything that is available at nominal cost. After a few years you can cancel the unnecessary subscriptions if you don't want them.

The forms you will receive are exceptionally valuable, particularly those which you receive from courts and administrative agencies. You will soon learn that when an agency or court makes a form available you'll be acting at your peril to use a different form or to make up your own form. Some civil service clerks are very definite in their opinion that there are two ways to do things, their way and the wrong way. In most cases you'll end up using their forms and recommended procedures, so you might just as well start that way and save yourself and your clients delay, expense, aggravation and embarrassment.

Commercial Sources

Free books, publications and forms are usually available from banks, insurance companies, title or escrow companies, trust companies, form printing companies, etc. Not only will you get free publications but you will also get some free lunches when the business development or sales representative calls on you to deliver the forms and books and wants to take you to lunch. As a new lawyer with 40 or 50 years of practice ahead of you, you are a very important potential source of business for these companies. The representatives know that as a new lawyer you can't send much business to them so there won't be any "hard sell." As you might expect, the banks' and trust companies' form books contain Will Forms and Trust Forms naming the sponsoring bank or trust companies as executor and trustees in the wills.

The life insurance companies' form books contain business buy/sell agreements for partnerships and corporations (funded with life insurance), pension and profit-sharing and retirement plans (also funded with life insurance), and question-and-answer questions about insurance taxation.

The title insurance companies and escrow companies have good forms for deeds and mortgages as well as good publications with highlights of real estate law.

The form printing companies will usually send a "sample kit" of forms available from them. Some of the companies charge for these sample kits.

More Expensive Books

When in doubt—don't. Law books are very expensive as is the maintenance. You should not buy one book that costs more than a few dollars during your first few years unless you know exactly what you are getting and unless you have a need for it. Use the law libraries of the courthouses, the law schools and other lawyers whenever you can.

The materials available vary from state to state. Depending on your state, and recognizing that lawyers differ as to what is best, I recommended obtaining your books in the following sequence:

1. Law dictionary
2. Unannotated codes or statutes (most recent edition)
3. Annotated codes or statutes
4. Legal encyclopedia (if available in your state)
5. Digest
6. Reporters
7. Specialized works
   a. Continuing eductation
   b. Pleading books
   c. Tax services
   d. Bankruptcy services
   e. Etc.

Use the Resources of Other Law Libraries

During your first few years of practice you'll have the time to go to the nearby law libraries including the libraries of nearby established law firms. These nearby firms will gladly make their libraries available when you explain that you are a new lawyer. In my opinion a good library is essential to doing complete, thorough, professional legal work. Most if not all lawyers with good law libraries feel the same way and will respect you for trying to do a thorough job. Using their library will enhance your reputation in the community—but *don't abuse your privileges*.

Follow these simple rules:

1. Never "drop in" to do research. Call first to ask if it's all right to come over "for a few minutes" (libraries are often in use as conference rooms, collating rooms, evidence rooms, etc.).

2. Be unobtrusive; remember you are a guest.

3. Don't interfere with other attorneys doing research. Be polite. Exchange a few pleasantries (introducing yourself to whoever is using the library at the same time). Ask if that person can suggest one or more works in the library which may help you, but don't let him or her do your research and don't let a friendly lawyer spend more than a few moments with you. Remember that person is being compensated by a client to do the client's work, not to do your work. It won't do you or the associate any good if a senior partner who has clients in the office and who is waiting for the research comes into the library and finds you and the associate in a "bull session" discussing college football teams.

4. Copying and photographing of books. If you must get a form or case or statute photocopied, offer to pay for the cost. If there is a reluctance to accept your money, ask the reproduction operator to take the money and to use it for the employees' coffee room. If the firm doesn't want the funds, offer to pay at the same rate charged by the local library. Your few dollars won't be needed by a firm which has a six-figure monthly overhead, but your desire not to be even a slight burden on your host will make a favorable impression and keep the doors open to you.

5. Clean up your mess before you leave. Put all books back. Clean out the ashtrays (whether or not you filled them) and straighten the chairs.

Subscriptions

In my opinion money spent on subscriptions to periodicals during your first few years of practice is a better investment than money spent on hardbound books. Generally speaking, such works fall into three categories:

A. What's new in the law.

B. How-to-do-it articles.

C. Scholarly research and writing.

A. *What's New in the Law.* These are the most improtant periodicals for you.

1. In law school you learned general legal theories, sometimes using cases 300 years old as teaching guides. You now must apply the principles to a specific factual situation in a modern context. Reading these periodicals will give you a good feeling for what is happening currently.

2. Clients and potential clients will be very impressed when you tell them about new laws and new cases which apply to them. They will be grateful that you are thinking of them.

3. Several of my cases in my early years were cases where another lawyer had told the clients that their case had no merit. In some of these cases the first attorney simply didn't know the current state of the law. By being aware of recent changes, I helped the clients and got devoted clients who many years later still brag to their friends and anyone who will listen about the "miracle attorney" who helped them when the other attorneys said the case was hopeless. This kind of client

will send you new clients as long as you live. (Wouldn't you if you were the client?)

4. You have no choice. If you don't keep up, you will soon be skilled in what the law used to be.

B. *How-To-Do-It Articles.* These articles are usually valuable to you for the forms and procedures they contain. If you have a problem in any area covered by the article you will save valuable time. Use of these articles is on a hit-and-miss basis. The best article on zoning won't be of much help if you never get a zoning matter. Unless you have a particular interest in a particular field it is my opinion that this type of publication should be deferred until you have been in practice two or three years.

C. *Scholarly Research and Writing.* If you have an interest in keeping up with the law reviews or journals of your particular law school and you want to subscribe and continue your subscription, then do so. Absent this motivation, I recommend against these types of periodicals. The cost simply isn't warranted in view of the probable uselessness early in a law career. This type of publication can be of great value in appellate briefs, but you probably won't have many cases going to appeal in your first few years. After you are established three or four years and can afford the luxury, you can subscribe to all those you care to, for example, textbooks with annual supplements.

Specific Types of Periodicals

A. *What's New in the Law.* The local legal newspaper for your community is a must. Advance sheets are also excellent. Bar journals of the American, state and local bar associations also contain excellent critiques on what is new in the law. If you wish to keep current in specific areas such as taxation, there are innumerable journals available such as the *Journal of Taxation.* Both Prentice-Hall and Commerce Clearing House have excellent weekly reports. Other areas of the law have similar journals.

B. *How-To-Do-It Articles.* Here again, bar journals and legal newspapers are excellent investments.

C. *Special Prices.* Most legal newspapers and bar associations have free or reduced prices for new admittees or for a trial period.

D. *Section Publications of the American Bar Association.* Bar Association Sections have excellent publications; however, they often are of limited value to a new practitioner with a "local" rather than national type of practice. It is difficult to generalize on these publications; the new attorney should carefully consider, however, which sections are likely to be of any use early in a career.

How to Buy Law Books

Book salesmen are sometimes less than candid in telling you how much law books cost. Keep in mind that most law books have three elements of cost:

1. Initial cost
2. Annual or more frequent upkeep for pocket parts or supplements
3. New volumes

A. *Initial Cost.* When you ask a book sales representative how much a set of books cost, you may hear double talk about "monthly payments" being small. Be insistent on knowing what the set costs.

B. *Annual Upkeep.* Insist on knowing what the annual cost of pocket parts or supplements is, based upon the most recent year's cost. Don't be put off by the sales rep answering your question by referring to the fact that this is "free" for one or two years. Remember, it won't be free after the first year or two.

C. *New Volumes.* Book publishers periodically replace old volumes with new volumes. They often do this when the pocket parts become too thick. Sometimes you'll still be paying off the old volumes when the new volumes get added to the bill. Perhaps you remember one or more instances in college of not being able to sell a used book at the end of the course due to a "new edition" (ofen with nondetectable changes except for the edition year); this is similar to new volume problems. Here again, the sales rep wants to talk about "low monthly payments." Try to negotiate a written guarantee that if a volume is replaced within a certain number of years, then you won't have to pay for the replacement volume.

How to Save Money Buying Used Law Books

A. *Law Schools and Law Libraries.* Let the librarian know you are interested in buying law books. These institutions are frequently the beneficiaries of inter vivos and testamentary gifts from lawyers or their widows. Often the set is a duplicate or triplicate of a set the law library already has. The library may be willing to sell you a set to use the cash for other purposes.

B. *Widows.* The estate of a deceased lawyer will usually want to sell the library.

C. *Mergers and Dissolutions.* When you receive notice or read about two firms getting together, you can call to see if there is an extra library for sale.

How Much to Pay for Used Books

You should be able to buy used books for 50 percent to 60 percent of the equivalent new book price. Obviously you may be willing to pay more or less depending upon the condition of the books and the urgency to sell or buy. Before buying be sure to check the age of the pocket parts, especially if the books have been around awhile. If you're not careful, the cost of your "bargain" and the cost of bringing the books up to date may be more than the cost of buying a new set.

Financing the Purchase

Although the book companies claim to sell you the books "interest free," you might do better borrowing money from the bank to buy the used books. Ask how much the cash price is to determine whether to use bank or publisher financiing.

The Cost of a Library

A very modest one- or two-lawyer library for an established firm costs between $6,000 and $10,000 per year (1984 prices) and therefore should not be purchased by the new lawyer.

How to Avoid Library Costs

A. Try to avoid library costs totally by affiliating with lawyers where there is already an existing library.

B. Courthouse law libraries. Judges have libraries and usually share with local lawyers.

How to Buy Law Books

The Federal Trade Commission issued its "Guide for the Law Book Industry" on August 18, 1975, because of abuses in the law book industry. An excellent in-depth article on the subject was written by Raymond M. Taylor and appears in the November 1975 issue of the *American Bar Association Journal.*

Before spending your hard-to-come-by dollars on a law book which you think you do need or will need, ask the following questions at a minimum:

1. *When was the book originally published and when was it last revised?* Is the book a 1983 reprint of a 1963 book with no updating? Be careful about books with copyrights from several years ago. It is difficult, if not impossible, to ascertain if the book is really current or is just the 1976 original with a few chapters modified to allow the publisher to claim it is a 1983 edition.

2. *Does the publisher plan a substantial revision* or replacement within a year or so, and if so, will you get some credit or refund for your nearly obsolete book?

3. *Does the title really reflect the contents?* Often titles are chosen with a view in mind to selling the book rather than describing the contents.

4. *Are supplements intended, and if so, what will they cost?* Be careful when a publisher won't commit to a maximum price on supplements in progress.

5. *What is the total price?*
   a. For cash.
   b. For installments.

Don't waste your time with a book company that won't give you an honest answer to an honest question. When the advertisement or the sales rep insists on talking about monthly payments instead of total price, you can assume they have something to hide.

6. *Are you sure you ordered or received the book?* You'll be surprised at how many bills you will receive for books you never ordered or never received. I suppose there is a thin line between "bookkeeping mistakes" and attempting to obtain money under false pretenses in some instances. Be very careful about paying for books.

7. *Do you understand the bill?* As you expand your library and incur a lot of monthly payments (it's unbelievable how fast they add up), your monthly bill will become very complex. The opportunities for "bookkeeping mistakes" are immense with large companies and their complex internal computer systems. If you don't understand the bill, don't pay it until you get a satisfactory explanation. Be sure that the bill conforms to your "deal" with the sales rep.

Saving Money on Postage

You may think that postage expense is beyond your control. This is not so. There are several things you can do to reduce postage expense.

Eliminate Postage Stamps

Postage stamps are commonly lost or stolen by employees, cleaning crews, etc.

1. *Outgoing mail.* Get the cheapest postage meter available. The meter will save you money. Postage meters can be rented on a monthly basis.

2. *Incoming mail.* Get a reply permit from the post office. (See details on following page.)

Get a Small Postage Scale

If you put too much postage on a letter, you'll waste the excess. On the other hand, if you don't put enough on, you may waste whatever you've used, if the recipient refuses to pay postage due and the letter is returned. Governmental agencies such as courts and sheriffs' departments ordinarily won't pay postage due. The delay in getting the mail back to you and out again may be detrimental and even fatal to your client's case and your malpractice liability.

You'll have many occasions to send out packages of documents. It is easy to waste money on excess and insufficient postage. Break the package into segments which can be weighed individually with the totals added together for the total cost of the package.

1. Go in person to the post office to fill out a form for Permit No.

2. Have envelopes printed (post office will give you samples).

3. For two or three months letter carrier will collect postage due when mail is delivered.

4. Your cost is regular postage plus five cents per item delivered to you (you pay 25 cents for 20 cents postage due).

5. After two or three months you can open a "Postage Due Account" with the post office and the postage due will be charged to your account without daily collection by letter carrier.

The principal advantage to this system is that you only pay for postage actually used. You don't spend money on stamps which clients never use and you don't risk employee theft or loss of postage. Although this seems expensive, it actually will save you money. Also your clients can immediately return their documents or payment checks to you.

Squeezing Extra Hours into the Day to Make More Money

If you can squeeze an extra 15 minutes a day into your billable day, this would translate into one and a fourth hours per week or about 60 hours per year, allowing for vacations, etc. At $50.00 per hour, this multiplies out to $3,000 per year at 15 minutes per day, or $6,000 per year at 30 minutes a day.

Here are some "tips" for squeezing extra time into the day.

1. *Keep a portable tape recorder in your car, in your home and in your brief case.* Whenever you get a "brilliant" idea concerning a case or a client, dictate it immediately and enter it into your time records when you get back to the office.

2. *Keep small note pads near your home telephone.* When a client calls you at home, make a note of the call on the pad, and enter the call on your time records when you get to the office. People sometimes call you at home, hoping to get free legal advice. When they see "telephone conference at home on Sunday re: mechanic's liens" on the bill, they will respect you for accuracy of your records. These notes may also protect you in a malpractice claim.

3. *Live as close as possible to your office.* In my entire professional career, I have never lived further than 15 minutes from my office. The difference between a 15-minute commute and a 45-minute commute is obviously five hours of chargeable time a week. In my early years, I frequently went home for dinner to see my children, and then returned to the office for an hour or two to work or for a meeting with clients.

4. *Don't waste your commuting time.* If you commute by public transportation, use the time for reading advance sheets and journals or listening to continuing education tapes.

Should You Hire a Secretary or Use a Secretarial Service?

Having a secretary on either a full-time or a part-time basis immediately available for your work is a luxury that you will not need initially. If you are in a suite with other lawyers, you may be able to borrow or buy a small amount of secretarial time from one of the lawyers who does not use a secretary's time fully.

I strongly recommend, however, that the new lawyer in practice contact the various secretarial services in the immediate neighborhood. You will find that these secretarial services will offer to the lawyer one or more of the following features:

A. Dictating equipment

B. Daily pick-up and delivery of finished work

C. A reasonable, minimum cost

D. A cost per word, or per line, over and above the minimum, based on actual usage

E. General familiarity with legal terminology.

Basically, the concept of a legal secretarial service is that you give the secretarial service a supply of your stationery. You then dictate all of your work into a tape recorder. (You could hand-write, if you wish, but this is not a good habit to get into.) The secretarial service will pick up your tapes at the end of the day. The next morning your dictated material has been typed and is ready for you.

For the first several months of your practice, when you have very little need for secretarial service, this is probably the most efficient and economical way for you to generate and handle secretarial work. Depending upon the particular secretarial service, you may be able to walk over there for a rush-rush emergency, and have them do it while you wait.

An additional side benefit of the use of secretarial service is the self-disciplining and good dictating habits which can be formed early in your career.

Due to the fact that you do not know who will be typing your particular work at the time, you must develop the habit of giving full and complete instructions when you dictate. In other words, you will not simply be able to say, "Send a letter to Mr. Jones." You will have to give specific instructions as to Mr. Jones' name, address, how many carbon copies or photocopies have to be made, etc. This giving of complete instructions for the secretarial service will be of invaluable assistance to you later in your professional career, when you dictate letters and documents for your own secretary, or for a secretarial pool.

I am not aware of any outside secretarial service using word processors or microcomputers with software packages. If you personally have the ability, you may be wise to use a microcomputer as a word processor instead of the traditional typewriter.

Dictating Equipment

Don't make any investment in dictating equipment until you have to. Use the dictating equipment supplied free by your outside secretarial service. Don't buy used dictating equipment unless it's been under warranty or maintenance contract. After you buy equipment, be sure to keep it under maintenance contract. Use only equipment which has a thumb-operated stop, dictate and reverse on the microphone handle. When you open your doors, get cheap portables for your car and briefcase. Get them cheap enough so that you can throw them away after a year or two and not feel badly. Footage meters are not necessary. Don't dictate tapes of more than five minutes' duration if you can help it. Secretaries get psychologically depressed by a 20- or 30-minute tape, but don't seem to mind 5- or 6-minute tapes.

Checklist for When You Start Secretarial and Nonlawyer Hiring

1. Get personnel manual—copy from *Lawyer's Handbook*.
2. Check with local high schools, junior colleges, business colleges and universities for trainee secretarial and clerical help who will work for free or low pay to get work training credits. Excellent source of trainees with intelligence.
3. Get "Secretarial Hiring Kits," to test basic skills from Wunderlich

of Northfield, Illinois; Minnesota Clerical Test; or Law Research Institute, Salt Lake City, Utah.

4. Get Leo Eisenstatt's *A Style Manual for the Law Office,* and plagiarize it. Available from American Bar Association, Order Fulfillment 511, 1155 E. 60th St., Chicago, IL 60637.

5. Allow three weeks for advertising and interviewing of applicants, and an additional two weeks notice which the successful candidate will have to give his or her present employer.

Should You Use
a Telephone Receptionist,
Telephone Exchange,
or Mechanical Answering Service?

Obviously, having your own secretary and/or telephone receptionist is nice. However, it may be a luxury that you can easily do without for the first several months. It is not likely that your phone is going to ring off the hook the first day, or even the first week, or possibly even the first month. After a couple of months, however, you can reasonably anticipate that you will have some telephone volume.

If you have an office in a suite with other lawyers, the receptionist is normally included in the cost of the suite.

As between using a telephone exchange, or a mechanical answering device, I strongly recommend the exchange. Try to find an exchange which services doctors and lawyers. These exchanges are experienced in handling emergency situations. They often are very well trained in calming the nervous or hysterical client until you can be contacted. From time to time, you should call your own number, to see what kind of service the exchange is giving your clients.

There is an expression which goes, "I needed you, I tried to get hold of you, I couldn't get hold of you, I don't need you any more." This is self-explanatory as to the necessity of having a good telephone exchange to handle your calls when you are at lunch, or during nights and weekends.

Currently, there is a trend for executives and professionals to answer their own telephone. I personally do not feel that this should be done in a law office. If you are with a client, you should not have to interrupt your interview or conference to answer a telephone. When I call a lawyer, and the lawyer answers the phone, I do not assume that the lawyer is following a modern trend. I assume the lawyer cannot afford someone to answer the phone. Therefore, I recommend against this practice. The problem with this type of telephone answering becomes obvious: You would have to tell one client to hold on so you can answer the other ringing telephone. Therefore, do not answer your own phones if you can possibly avoid it. Even if you have to bring in your spouse or a friend to answer the phones for you, in my opinion, this is preferable to your answering your own telephones.

How to Answer the Phone

Volumes have been written on how to answer the phones. I recommend that the phone be answered as follows: "Good morning, Carolyn Jones' office. This is Mary Moore speaking. Can I help you?" We use this method and get many compliments from clients.

Why You Should Use Investigators

As soon as possible after opening your office, ask several lawyers for recommendations for investigators. Meet with a few of them and choose one who really seems to want your business.

Investigators cost money, but they cost relatively little compared to what they will earn for you and your client or save you and your client.

When you tell your client that his or her case requires investigators and that investigators cost money, the client will be more than willing to pay you money "up front." The client will also be impressed by your professionalism. There will be a confidence that the case is being handled properly.

Investigators have the proper photographic equipment and recording equipment. They seem to have "friends" in place where you can only get a closed door. They know how to interview witnesses and to follow up leads. I've often gotten good settlements on cases by showing the insurance adjuster my investigator's reports and asking to see theirs.

As a new lawyer you'll need the investigator's help in evaluating the case. They've seen hundreds of cases and are more skilled than you in most of the areas in which they work.

Within limits, investigators will work with you on payment, sometimes deferring part or all of their fee until the case settles. Never let an investigator or any other witness testify who is owed money by you or your client. Their testimony may be weakened due to a suspicion that their compensation is predicated on the results of the case.

Part VII
Resources and Advice

Where to Go for Help

Most lawyers reading this will have almost no knowledge of how to manage a law practice. Therefore, you should increase your knowledge immensely just by reading this one publication.

This publication should go a long way towards getting you started in the creation and building of your law practice.

This book is only intended to get you started. You will soon find that you need more resources than are available here.

When I first decided to write this book I spent several hours in a university law library looking for sources of materials for new lawyers. I then had one of my law clerks spend weeks going through the sources that I had found, plus finding additional sources I had missed.

Shortly after spending a lot of time and effort, I discovered Robert P. Bigelow's list, which is the best I've ever seen and far better than mine for both new and established lawyers.

Mr. Bigelow's article is contained in the Fall 1975 issue of *Legal Economics,* which can be obtained from the ABA Section of Economics of Law Practice, 750 N. Lake Shore Drive, Chicago, Illinois, 60611. This issue also contained an excellent article on preparing your staff manual.

Join the American Bar Association's Section of Economics of Law Practice and receive *Legal Economics;* consult back issues, which you can identify by using LOIS (Law Office Information Service). On balance, *Legal Economics* will be an investment, not an expense.

There are many good publications available. As with the law library, it's a question of balancing the value of the publication to a new lawyer against the expenditure of cash, which is in short supply to the new lawyer.

This book is intended to teach basics, which do not ordinarily change radically in a short time. However, law office management and administration is now mushrooming as a profession, and there are major changes occurring due to technological advances in word processing, computers, communication, document reproduction, etc.

Therefore, until you are established, as a general rule, you should stay away from hard-bound publications which may become rapidly obsolete and dated, and as a general rule, you should concentrate on periodicals during your first few years.

The following are recommended to you in the first years. Prices are approximate.

1. *Legal Economics*. American Bar Association. 750 N. Lake Shore Drive, Chicago, Illinois 60611 (bimonthly/via membership in the Economics of Law Practice Section, ABA, which includes a subscription).

2. *The Practical Lawyer*. 4025 Chestnut Street, Philadelphia, Pennsylvania 19104 (eight times per year/$15 per year).

3. *Case and Comment*. Lawyers Cooperative Publishing Company, Aqueduct Building, Rochester, New York 14603 (free).

4. *Barrister*. Publication of Young Lawyers Section, American Bar Association, 750 N. Lake Shore Drive, Chicago, Illinois 60611 (quarterly/via membership in the Young Lawyers Division, ABA, which includes a subscription).

Thus, for a fairly nominal sum, you can get some "upgrading" of what is in this book.

When you have been in practice a few years and your practice is booming, you and/or your office manager can get more deeply into what is then current with one or more of the following (prices approximate):

1. *Law Office Economics and Management*. Callaghan and Company, Chicago, Illinois (monthly/$55 per year).

2. *Lawyers Newsletter*. Law Publications, Inc., Los Angeles, California (bimonthly/$18 per year).

3. *Manual for Managing the Law Office*. Prentice-Hall, Englewood Cliffs, New Jersey ($99 per year).

4. *How to Manage Your Law Office*. Matthew Bender & Company, New York, New York ($38.50 for the book, plus annual supplements at unknown cost).

Books, Pamphlets, etc.

I hesitate to recommend a book today that may be obsolete or out of print by the time you need it; however, I strongly recommend that you keep current on those materials available through the Monograph Series and other publications of the American Bar Association Economics of Law Practice Section. For a relatively few dollars you can have a library which is up to date, with systems which in most cases are easily adaptable to your office.

Courses, Conferences, Etc.

It should be kept in mind that there are many opportunities during the year to attend programs and workshops put on by various organizations. Some of these have a service to the profession aspect. A little careful planning will enable you to combine these programs with your vacations, getting at least a partial income tax deduction for the travel expenses involved. See chapter on "The Importance of Continuing Education."

The Importance of
Continuing Education

If on January 1 of a given year you know all the law there is to know in any typical area of law, and if for one year you make no attempt to "keep current," at the end of the year you will be an expert on what the law used to be. You went to law school to learn legal principles and to spot legal issues. If you learned well, your legal education will probably last you about five years. You must keep up with the law.

The First Two or Three Years of Your Practice

There are many courses and seminars offered by universities and various institutes. In the main, these courses are too expensive for the new lawyer and often are not suited to your needs. The costs run as much as several hundred dollars. The basic courses are too far below your level of experience, and the sophisticated courses are too far above your level of experience. In some states, the state university with the state bar puts on low-cost programs with excellent textbooks. Fees of $35.00 to $50.00 for a two- or three-hour program, including the book, are reasonable and worth the price. Therefore, although continuing education is important, getting it cheaply can be difficult. In my opinion, the cheapest and easiest ways to keep current are as follows:

1. *Daily Legal Newspaper.* These papers are often free or low cost your first three to six months. They normally contain cases of interst to practicing lawyers.

2. *Bar Association Committee Luncheons and Programs.* You can get the benefits of experienced attorneys' views and help for the price

of a luncheon or an hour or two out of the office.

3. *Bar Association Journals.* The state and local bar journals are excellent low-cost sources of new legislation and major cases as well as "How-to-Do-It" articles.

4. *Audio Tapes.* Audio tapes run anywhere from a few dollars to $20 or $30 for a one-hour tape. The only advantage to audio tapes, in my opinion, is that you can listen to them in places where it's not practical to read, such as your automobile on the freeway.

Unfortunately, many tape performances are dull and boring. The panelists or speakers often read prepared papers into a microphone with all the emotion and feeling of a log. The tapes sometimes constitute a traffic hazard by putting you to sleep on the freeway. I frankly don't like audio tapes but suggest that you try a few and form your own opinion.

The audio tapes are normally available from or through various state bar associations as well as through other commercial sources. The bar journals will usually contain information on the availability of the tapes.

5. *Video Tapes.* Excellent video tapes are available from varied sources on varied subjects. The commercial tapes are normally best because they use speakers who are interesting as well as informative. The American Bar Association Economics of Law Practice Section video tapes, for example, use only entertaining speakers.

University tapes and local bar association tapes are often a waste of time and money because you can't stay awake for the dull, boring speaker.

You could make your own video tapes for training lawyers and secretaries, and for informing clients. Additionally, you can "write off" or deduct for income tax purposes video equipment that you use in your practice.

After Two or Three Years

1. *Non-Practice Areas.* After you have been out of school two or three years, you will have started your downhill decline in those areas in which you haven't had any practice. Therefore, some of the institutes and seminars which would have been below you right out of law school are no longer below you and are worth the expense if you want to keep some familiarity with the area.

2. *Practice Areas.* If you are, in fact, doing some work in the sub-

ject area of the seminar or institute, then these courses are worth their weight in gold. You *must,* however, undertake the courses with the proper perspective. In most courses, you should already know 85% to 95% of the material *before* you attend. Your purpose in attending should be to pick up a few "pointers" or tips. I've never yet attended a seminar where I didn't pick up one or two tips or techniques.

I've traveled thousands of miles and spent thousands of dollars to attend seminars and institutes that lasted from one to five days. I've never been disappointed because I maintained the proper perspective. To put it another way, if you don't know 85 percent to 95 percent of what you'll hear before you get there, then perhaps you're not as sharp as you think you are.

Follow the Leaders

If you don't believe that continuing education is important, look about you when you go to a program. You'll see the "specialists" and lead lawyers in the big law firms. They know the importance and value of continuing education.

Getting Maximum Tax Dollar From Your Educational Expenses

Amounts spent to maintain your skills as a lawyer are deductible for income tax purposes, including transportation, meals and lodging away from home as well as the tuition charges.

With a little careful planning, you can combine your educational expenses with a rest away from your office. Courses today are offered on cruise ships and resorts as well as in hotels and classrooms. Another advantage in attending courses away from home is the opportunity to meet lawyers from other areas of the state or country who can give you new or different approaches or perspectives in areas you deal with. From time to time, you may get some referral business from these lawyers, but this should be a minor factor in attending the program.

The Wheel Has Been Invented

At several places in this book I have emphasized that as far as the new lawyer is concerned, the basic principles of starting and building a law practice remain constant over the years. I spent a lot of time and money and made a lot of mistakes learning the lessons I've tried to teach you in this book. This book simply attempts to put the things a new lawyer in practice has to know into one place.

This book has been written over a period of more than a year, and updated over a period of eight years. I've written parts of it on airplanes and in hotel rooms on five continents. On one trip to Morocco and Kenya, I met John P. Clark, a lawyer from Winslow, Arizona. John was interested in this book and told me about an incident that occurred in 1932. An itinerant book seller approached John in 1932 and offered to show him how to increase his income for a $5.00 fee. Things were bad during the depression and Winslow, Arizona, was no exception, so John paid the $5.00.

The sales rep printed up some forms and gave them to John for the $5.00 fee, telling him to fill out the form at the end of the interview and to give it to the client with the charge filled in. A copy of the form was placed in the client file. (A copy of the form follows this chapter.)

In 1975, I spent six months and $25,000 to program a $40,000 in-house computer for billing. The Missouri Bar Survey was made in 1964. The American Bar Survey was done in 1980. On reflection I'm not sure that my computer or the Missouri Survey or the American Bar Survey has given us much new information that wasn't sold for $5.00 by the itinerant book seller in Winslow, Arizona, in 1932.

LAW OFFICES
JOHN P. CLARK
ATTORNEY AT LAW
WINSLOW, ARIZONA

CLIENT'S LEGAL ADVICE MEMO

CLIENT—

FACTS BY CLIENT—

DATE—

ARRIVAL—

DEPARTURE—

FEE—

LAW AS READ—
   SEE _____

OPINION BY ATTY.—

Handwritten original is given to client at end of interview, two copies kept by lawyer, one for accounts receivable, one for client file.

What Are the Consequences of "Violating" the "Canons" of Professional Ethics or the Code of Professional Responsibility?

This is a difficult question to answer. The answer depends upon the particular "violation" and upon your licensing laws.

1. A brief review of some basic definitions will be helpful.

A. *"Bar association"* usually means a *voluntary* group of lawyers. Associations are normally organized on a geographic basis and may be on an international, national, state, county, city or neighborhood basis. A state or local bar association may have its own "canons" or "code," or it may adopt *in toto* or by reference the canons or codes of another association. In some states, the bar association can "recommend" a license proceeding against a lawyer.

B. *"State bar"* usually means a mandatory bar group that you must belong to to practice law in the state. This type of bar is often called an "integrated bar" (having nothing to do with civil rights) or a "uniform bar." "State bars" can sometimes do more or less than "bar associations."

C. *"Canons of Professional Ethics"* are the pronouncements of the American Bar Association adopted in 1908 which remained in effect until 1970.

D. *"Code of Professional Responsibility."* The Code contains the Canons, Ethical Considerations and Disciplinary Rules. There are nine Canons which are general statements, and these are subdivided into 128 Ethical Considerations and 39 Disciplinary Rules. The Code was adopted in 1970. The Code of Professional Responsibility can be obtained free from the American Bar Association, 750 N. Lake Shore Drive, Chicago, Illinois, 60611.

E. *Rules of Professional Conduct.* These are rules promulgated by licensing bodies such as the supreme court or legislature of a state.

2. With some of the definitions in mind, we can go back to the basic question of the effect of violation of the Code.

The Code, in my opinion, represents the sincere efforts of well-meaning experts to develop standards of conduct for lawyers on the highest level for the benefit of the public. Some of the rules may not be practical or enforceable and there are other objections. Notwithstanding all of the criticisms of the Code, on balance, it is a good work and deserving of respect and following.

The new lawyer should not be frightened or awed by the Code. Violations of some of the provisions will cost you your license. Violations of other provisions could result in disciplinary proceedings such as a reprimand or being expelled from the association.

Is unethical conduct *per se* also illegal? Some unethical conduct can be illegal, such as trust fund violations or fee splitting with the laity, and could result in criminal prosecution as well as disciplinary proceedings. Some unethical conduct could result in disciplinary proceedings only, such as telephone book advertising violations. Some violations probably have absolutely no effect in some states, such as fee splitting.

In summary, "violating" the Code of Professional Responsibility can have either serious consequences or lesser consequences, depending upon whether the Code is or is not part of your disciplinary system and upon the powers of your state bar or bar association.

As a new lawyer, you do not have enough sophistication or experience to decide selectively not to observe portions of the Code. You should initially observe the Code in its entirety, both in letter and in spirit. When you are an established attorney and better understand the needs of the public, you can and should attempt to modify the local application of the Code to meet the local needs of the public.

Remember that, even if you do not lose your license to practice law, expulsion from a bar association can leave an ugly stain on your career and can cost you money by loss of referrals.

I must strongly advise that you thoroughly understand exactly what the situation is in your state or community *before* you begin your practice. If you've in sole practice there is no one to review your work and you may be inadvertently doing something unethical, without realizing it. Somewhere in your legal education you were taught or exposed to legal ethics. Be sure you understand the interrelation of ethics and licensing.

How to Manage and
Collect Accounts Receivable

Effective management and collection of your accounts receivable is critical for any lawyer, but especially for the new lawyer.

What Is an Account Receivable?

Very simply, an account receivable is money people owe you for work done or costs advanced *after* you have sent them a bill. Until you send a bill, you don't have an account receivable. You have work in process or, if you wish to be fancy, you can call it deferred time, or unrelieved time, or any other number of fancy titles, but it is not an account receivable until after you send a bill.

Professional credit managers have written volumes of information on this subject. In this chapter I'll try to convey what a lawyer, especially a new lawyer without formal training in accounts receivable collection or management, has to know. Although this chapter may appear lengthy, it contains only the bare minimum of what you have to know.

Reasons for Accounts Receivable Management

1. *Your Own Cash Flow*. You can't pay bills at home or in the office with warm feelings and professional satisfaction. You need cash. Landlords, secretaries, book sellers, supermarkets, auto repair shops, stationery supply stores, credit card companies, etc., all will insist on cash for payment. The best source of cash is "cash up front." The second best source is your accounts receivable.

2. *To recognize the danger signs at the earliest possible point for*

those cases and clients which are or may become problem cases for any number of reasons. Sometimes people don't pay because they can't, or think they can't. Sometimes they don't pay because they don't want to pay. In either case, you may have a problem which can only get worse as time goes on. Your client may be dissatisfied with you or with the way the case is being handled. In either case, you had better find out as soon as possible.

Sometimes a client simply ignores the bill rather than tell you of his or her dissatisfaction. You must find out what is wrong.

3. *To have facts upon which to decide to terminate the professional relationship when the client refuses to pay the bill.* It is better to say: "Mr. Jones, you now owe $775. You still need $2,500 more work. You haven't paid anything since March when you paid $50 and before that, December, when you paid $100. I'm asking if possibly we should make an arrangement or terminate the case," than it is to say: "Mr. Jones, your bill is overdue. And if you don't pay, I can't work."

4. *To keep your bad receivable losses as low as possible.* Every business and profession has some bad accounts receivable. You can't avoid them (unless you only work for cash up front). The secret is to keep them as low as possible and to prevent small losses from becoming big losses.

5. *Because every dollar of accounts receivable is 100 percent profit or loss.* Collecting an account receivable is 100 percent profit and not collecting it is 100 percent loss. It is right on the bottom line. Your income as a lawyer is heavily dependent on your not having bad accounts receivable.

I have practiced as a CPA and as a lawyer for a quarter of a century. I've lost more money on uncollected receivables for good work done than I've lost because a contingency case was lost or because the case was a bad case.

Definitions

1. *Bill.* The bill is the document you send wherein you first inform the client that you did the work or advanced the costs and that you expect payment *now!* The bill is the *first* communication asking for money for work previously done. The bill might be for a period of time (monthly, etc.), or for a quantity of work done (stages in a proceeding), or work to be done in the future.

2. *Billing.* Billing is the *process* of preparing and sending the bill.

3. *Statement.* A statement is the document you send *after* you send the first bill and you are still owed all or part of what you asked for on the first bill. In some cases there will be an overlapping or combining of the statement where you ask for money for work previously billed and a new bill where you ask for money for the first time for new work or costs.

4. *Account Receivable.* What the client owes you after you have sent a bill.

5. *Work in Progress.* A case or matter that is not completed and not ready for billing (probate, contingency case, etc.).

6. *Deferred Time.* The work is done. You could bill the client, but you don't want to just yet. (The case will be over next month and you'll send a final bill, or the client is temporarily upset with the bill and it's better to wait, etc.)

7. *Delinquent.* It is easier for me to give an example than to explain. The time sequence is as follows:
   a. Send Bill no. 1 for work done or to be done (at this point not delinquent).
   b. Send Bill no. 2 for additional or different work done or to be done along with statement for first bill unpaid (at this point still not delinquent).
   c. Send Bill no. 3 for new or additional work done or to be done along with statement for first bill unpaid in whole or in part. *You now have a delinquent account receivable which demands immediate attention.*

Note that I have defined "delinquent" in terms of the number of times you have told the client you wish payment rather than in terms of days, weeks, or months.

8. *Accounts Receivable Listing.* A list of all accounts receivable, normally in alphabetical order.

9. *Accounts Receivable Aging.* A list of all accounts receivable normally showing a "spread" of amounts due by time periods (often combined with a listing).

10. *Priority Accounts Receivable List.* These are the 10 or 15 largest receivables and must be reviewed weekly. These are important clients who must be monitored continually as to whether they are current or delinquent.

11. *Delinquent Accounts Receivable.* This is a case where you and the client have a problem which must be faced. (See definition of "delinquent.")

How to Analyze and Use Account Receivable Information

1. Get the information on *all* accounts receivable *monthly* so you can, in a timely manner, recognize the problems that are developing and have developed. Normally, you get this information when you do billings.

2. Get the information on your *ten* most serious problems (if you have that many) *weekly* so you don't forget about them or lose sight of their importance.

3. Always get your accounts receivable information in terms of dollar size, not in terms of alphabetical listing. Pay the most attention to the "biggest," whether or not it is delinquent. Always be aware of whom your major debtors are so you can respond accordingly.

4. Define what a "delinquent" account is for your purposes. I have my own definition which I consider a "softie" approach, but which works. (See definition no. 11 above.)

5. Decide whether or not you can continue working on the case without payment and, if you can, under what arrangement.

6. Contact client. (See How to Collect Accounts Receivable section below.)

   a. First contact: short note from secretary, bookkeeper or office manager.
   b. Second contact: telephone call from you to client.
   c. Third contact: letter from you to client setting forth telephone call summary.

7. Decide whether this would be an appropriate time to allow client to make some other lawyer rich before you get in deeper.

8. Consider refunding all money paid by client as fees to get out of a bad case before it becomes a serious case. It is better to refund $750 and not collect $1,500 more than it is to do $3,000 more of work you'll never get paid for because the client can't or won't pay.

9. *Never forget* you are your client's lawyer, not the client's partner. You have no obligation, moral or legal, to go under financially just because your client is going under or can't or won't pay for services. Legal aid does exist. There is nothing wrong with your budgeting a percentage of your time for *pro bono* work, but you, and not the client, must decide when you can do *pro bono* work.

How to Manage Accounts Receivable

You manage accounts receivable by getting the proper information and then *acting* on that information. Simply knowing about your accounts receivable isn't adequate if you don't *do* something about them. Obviously, you can't do something about them if you don't have the information.

Information Needed

To maintain a simple, effective account receivable management system, you must have the following information *before* contacting a client:

1. How much all of your clients owe you.
2. How much a client owes on this matter.
3. How much a client owes on other matters.
4. How much work (in dollars) has been done.
5. How much work (in dollars) remains to be done and over what period of time.
6. History of payments made (especially dates and amounts of last two payments).
7. When you last discussed fees with the client and what the client said and what you said (you should have a memo to the file on this).
8. What your fee agreement (preferably in writing) requires the client to do and whether or not the client is in default on the agreement.
9. Other factors (client sent you a $25,000 case, or is the brother-in-law of the president of your best corporate client), etc.
10. The priority accounts receivable list. These are the biggest accounts receivable you have (typically 10 to 15) and warrant review at least once a week.
11. The delinquent accounts receivable list. These are the accounts receivable which are delinquent.
12. The action accounts receivable list. These are the delinquent receivables which require immediate action. (Don't waste time on a $300 receivable when someone is delinquent $2,200.)

How to Collect Accounts Receivable (Accounts Receivable Collection Technique in Chronological Sequence)

1. Have the bookkeeper sign and send a short note included with the bill but not typed on the bill to the effect, "It has come to our attention that your account is overdue. If there is a problem, please call me."

2. Have the secretary or bookkeeper call client's bookkeeper or accounts payable person. Be helpful, not threatening: "We notice that your May account of $_____ has not been paid and I'd like to know what to tell Mr. Foonberg." Write down the response.

3. Always send the bill to both a company name and a person's name. People don't like seeing their own name on an unpaid bill.

4. The attorney should call the client and say something to the following effect: "Joe, I'm very concerned that our bill is being ignored and we're wondering if there is a problem with you. You owe $_____. Nothing has been paid since _____ and there's more work to be done and we want to know what you want to do."

Say nothing more. No matter how long the silence, no matter how awkward the silence, say nothing more. The next move is up to the client.

5. Get a commitment. "I'll send you $_____ by _____ and $_____ every week thereafter."

6. Send a letter to the client confirming the new arrangment to be sure there is no misunderstanding.

7. If the client refuses to make a commitment, begin the process of dropping the client.

8. Try to match the client's payment to you with the client's income (pay days, contract closing, etc.).

9. If you have a loser, face up to the fact as soon as possible and begin to devote your energies more to the clients who honor their agreements.

10. Remember "Foonberg's Rule"—it is better not doing the work and not getting paid than doing the work and not getting paid.

11. Every lawyer should do some *pro bono* work, but the lawyer, not the clients, should decide which clients don't pay.

12. The *billing* is the *process* of preparing and sending the bill.

13. A *statement* is the *document* where you ask for money after you have sent the first bill. In some cases you will be overlapping.

    a. Send bill—*not* delinquent.

    b. Send statement following the month with first bill unpaid— *be aware* that a problem may be developing.

    c. Send statement the following month with first bill unpaid. You have a problem which demands immediate attention.

14. Decide whether or not you can continue working on the case without payment and, if you can, under what arrangement.

15. Contact client.

Where to Get Cost-Effective Help to Build and Expand Your Practice

As far as I'm aware, *How to Start and Build a Law Practice* was the first book devoted to building a law practice. In 1968 when I began doing programs on starting and building a law practice, the subject was considered to be unethical. There was objection to using law school facilities for such programs and we held them in the basement of a savings and loan. The county bar association refused to announce the availability of the programs to new admittees because they thought it was unethical. I had to print the first copies of the first edition of this book at my own expense, because its subject matter was considered controversial and possibly unethical.

Today the world has changed. Bar associations and law schools and national and international organizations now invite me to speak and lead workshops on practice development. *How to Start and Build a Law Practice* is the all-time best seller of the American Bar Association and is deemed a classic. I was told that the Law School Library Association has classified this book as the title most stolen from law school libraries in the U.S.A.

There are now many self-styled experts on practice development. There are now also other books on the subject. Some of these books have some value. There are also "consultants" who will help you design a firm brochure, or TV advertising or other media advertising. Public relations experts will get your photo on the society pages. Other experts will tell you how to dress, what art work to hang in your office, etc. There are experts who will lead "in-house" marketing seminars or workshops for your firm. There are universities which provide seminars and lectures on lawyer marketing. There are periodicals on lawyer marketing.

I list the foregoing sources not to recommend them but to advise you that they exist in the event you wish to buy them. In the main I advise great caution in using them for the following reasons:

1. They are normally directed toward the larger firm which has an established practice and which has lots of time and money to invest. They often are not responsive to smaller firms and sole practitioners. Those techniques which work for a small firm or sole practitioner are normally applicable to larger firms but not vice versa.

2. They require a large cash outlay *now* and promise long-term cash results *later.* New lawyers and sole practitioners and small firms can't afford that impact on cash flow.

3. They are excellent in helping you self-inventory your problems and self-define your goals, but they don't help you solve your problems or give you the techniques and tools you need to actually get results. (It has been said that a consultant borrows your watch to tell you what time it is and breaks your watch in the process.) They often stir up ambition and desire but leave you unfulfilled in terms of the end-product needed.

4. At the risk of being immodest, I am recommending to you a book that is not available as of the time of the updating of this book. It will be cost-effective and immediately usable for every lawyer in America, especially the sole practitioner and small firms that have limited cash, but need immediate results. It will be published in the near future. It was written by me and took more than five years to write because of the rapid changes in defining permissible and non-permissible practice development methods.

This new book is based on three sources:

1. What I have learned from doing more than 300 programs and workshops for tens of thousands of practicing lawyers (as well as doctors, architects, dentists, small businesses, etc.) in almost every state in the Union and many foreign countries over a period of almost two decades. Most of these programs were done at bar association conventions where I got input from lawyers from all over the United States or from the specific states. My input is literally from every possible type and size of law practice.

2. Those things which I have applied in my own practice and which are successful.

3. Those things which I have advised others to do which worked in their practices as reported in their unsolicited reports to me over the years.

The new book which I am recommending will be entitled *How To Get and Keep Good Clients,* subtitled "Practice Development and Lawyer Marketing Techniques for the Sole Practitioner and Small Law Firm."

How to Get and Keep Good Clients assumes an existing practice. This book, *How to Start and Build a Law Practice,* devotes itself to both management and entry-level practice development. It assumes a starting point of zero experience. Most of the work, then, has to be done by the lawyer and indeed can be done by the lawyer prior to opening the doors. This book also provides a master plan where all of the actualities are integrated. The basic concepts and lessons of *How to Start and Build a Law Practice* would apply to any lawyer in America.

Much of the work detailed in my new book, *How to Get and Keep Good Clients,* can be done and indeed should be done by either non-lawyers or by lawyers. *How to Get and Keep Good Clients* uses some of the same fundamental concepts as *How to Start and Build a Law Practice* but recognizes that the existing law practice has the demands of clients and staff members and family members co-existing with the desire to get and keep better clients. Each of the techniques in *How to Get and Keep Good Clients* can be applied one at a time in any sequence that the particular lawyer wishes to implement. Many of the techniques can be used or not used by an individual lawyer, depending on whether or not he or she feels comfortable with the technique. There is no need for every lawyer in the firm to do the same thing at the same time. Those who are comfortable utilizing the most number of techniques will become the better "client-getters." Others may still remain good technicians, as their success or failure may not be dependent on client-getting abilities. *How to Get and Keep Good Clients* also assumes a practice-experience frame of reference so that the individual lawyer can understand why some prior activities were successful and some were not successful.

Although there is a small amount of common ground in the two books, I recommend that every lawyer should have both books and periodically should re-read each.

How to Get and Keep Good Clients will be the most cost-effective practice development investment you can make.

The Importance of
Doing It Right

My very first client was the man who installed my telephone. He installed my telephone at the end of March. He looked on the wall and saw my CPA license. He told me that he had prepared his own income tax return and would like me to review it for $5.00. In those days $35.00 was a reasonable minimum fee for an income tax return. I told him that I would need about an hour of his time for an interview to ascertain whether the income tax return was correct. He begged me to please look it over for $5.00 and he wouldn't hold me responsible for any mistakes. I told him that I wouldn't do anything unless I did it right and that $35.00 was my minimum fee. He said he wouldn't pay that much and we talked about something else until he finished his work.

Two days later the phone rang and it was the installer. I said hello and told him that the phone was working fine because my wife had already called twice. He said he was calling me for professional help and would I see him that evening in the restaurant of the building. I asked him the nature of the problem. He explained that his wife had a daughter by a prior marriage and that the father was a drunken bum. He had promised the wife that if anything happened to her, he would do his best to keep the child away from the natural father. He had not adopted the child. His wife had just died in an accident and he wanted to keep the child from the natural father.

I discussed the case with a couple of lawyers in the building who told me the case was an absolute loser because the natural father would get the child unless it could be conclusively proven that the father was unfit. They also told me that in those days $2,500 would be a reasonable fee and to be sure to get $2,500 for investigators, deposition costs, child psychiatrists, etc.

I met the client that night in the restaurant and told him that he had a losing case and not to waste his money, and that I needed my fee and costs paid in advance before I would begin work. Truthfully, I was trying to dissuade him from proceeding with the case. He told me he had already been to see another lawyer who told him essentially the same thing but who was a little more optimistic and who would charge less. I said nothing. He said he would drop by the next morning.

The next morning he came by with a cashier's check for $2,500 and 14 $100 bills and asked if I could wait a few days for the next $1,100. As a phone company employee he had accumulated a large amount of AT&T stock and was borrowing against it to get money for my fees. I could have waited six months.

I then got cold feet and told him that I had never handled this type of case before and in fact had never handled any kind of case before. He told me that he knew this was my first time but that he had promised his wife that if anything happened to her he would do his best. He said that I had told him when I refused to do his tax return for $5.00 that I wouldn't do anything unless I did it right. Therefore he was confident that even though the case was a loser and I had no prior experience, I would do whatever could be done and he would have fulfilled his promise to his late wife.

I won the case (by default) after lining up all sorts of witnesses and devoting all of my time day and night to the case. The other lawyer caved in when he and his client saw the huge array of evidence I had prepared.

I got a $2,500 fee on the custody case, and a $3,000 fee on his wife's industrial accident case, all within a short time of opening my practice, because I turned down a low fee and told a prospective client that I wouldn't do something unless I did it right.

Believe me, over the years you'll do better and get more clients and fees if you make it clear that you'll only do things the right way. Always do your best. Even when you underestimate the fee, do your best. When the client is not worthy of your best, give your best anyway.

Checklist for Opening
Your First Law Office

Foreword

This is a checklist for opening a law office. It was initially prepared in 1979 at the request of the Young Lawyers Division of the American Bar Association through its then President, David Weiner of Cleveland, Ohio, and its then Economics of Law Practice Section Representatives, Kenneth Rice, of Everett, Washington, and Karen Feyerherm of Seattle, Washington. Sam Smith of Miami Beach, Florida, then Chairman of the American Bar Association's Economics of Law Practice Section, encouraged its preparation and Bob Wilkins of Columbia, South Carolina, gave me valuable suggestions and advice as he has so often done in the past. Bill Blaine of the California Continuing Education of the Bar was most helpful in suggesting its dissemination by CEB. Curt Karplus, Assistant Director of CEB, served as editor.

This list is as comprehensive as I can make it based upon my experiences in doing programs for young lawyers throughout the United States and Canada and as Chairman of the New Lawyers in Practice Committee of the American Bar Association. I welcome your comments, and suggestions for revisions.

Make a Timetable and a Priority Checklist

After learning of the approximate lead time you'll need for each step in the checklist, make a priority checklist. Do the things first that will require the longest time. This checklist reflects upon my experiences with the difficulties in decision-making and getting things done. The things requiring the most lead time should be at the top of your list;

the things that require less lead time should be toward the bottom. You will have to rearrange many of the items into your own list, depending on your personal situation and local circumstances.

Consider the Area in Which You Wish to Practice

1. Where are your friends and relatives?
2. Pick a growing rather than decaying area. Watch out for blight and decay. Consider possible changes in economic patterns due to escalating energy costs.
3. Do you want an urban, rural or suburban practice? Analyze whether you can really be happy in a rural or small town atmosphere or in an urban atmosphere. This is a matter of your personality and background

Consider Quality of Life Factors

1. *Quality of professional life:* What kinds of cases and clients can you expect to get where you will practice?
2. *Quality of social life:* Do you want proximity to museums, symphonies, discos, young intellectual people, etc.?
3. *Quality of atmosphere:* Is there smog and pollution, or clean air and water?
4. *Quality of recreational life:* Do you want proximity to swimming, skiing, boating, hiking, hunting, etc.?
5. *Quality of home life:* Is the area safe for your spouse and children? Will you be afraid to go out at night or to sleep with the windows open?
6. *Quality of economic life:* What kind of money can you earn there?

Consider Miscellaneous Factors

1. Proximity of office to public transportation for staff and clients.
2. Proximity to eating places for client entertainment and meetings.
3. Proximity to law library.
4. Proximity to major anticipated clients.
5. Type of practice you are planning. For personal injury, workers' compensation, and criminal law, proximity to courts and administrative hearing locations or jails may be important.
6. Proximity to other lawyers for possible consultation, referral of overflow work or library sharing.

7. Will office and building be accessible for people on crutches or in wheelchairs, or elderly people?

What Size Office Will You Need?

You'll need 400 to 600 square feet of office space per lawyer, as follows: personal office, 150 to 200 square feet (smaller is OK if you have access to a conference room for meetings with clients); secretarial area, 150 to 200 square feet (try to defer this for a few months, if possible); reception area, storage, copy machine, etc., 100 to 200 square feet.

Consider Office Sharing

Office sharing can be very economical. Shared suites are becoming common. You give up some individuality, but you save a lot of agonizing and decision-making. It is obviously cheaper to divide costs for receptionist, library, reception area and furniture, secretary, photocopy equipment, conference rooms, etc. You also have access to experienced lawyers for assistance and possibly some referral work. Ask the lawyers already in the suite how long they have been in the suite and what they like or dislike about the arrangement. Be careful to control your own phone number.

Consider Cheap Space in an Expensive Building

Inside, non-window space is very cheap. With imaginative drapes, lighting and decorating, the client won't realize that the offices are inside offices. Cost savings in rent can be very significant. Indicate that you are willing to accept inside space for price or other considerations.

Make Contacts to Find Space

Helpful sources of information include your local legal newspaper, nonlegal local papers and local bar association journals. A commercial broker may be a good source, if the space you require is not too small. Other lawyers can be of assistance. If there is a particular building in which you want space, try a form letter sent or delivered to every existing tenant and to the building manager. This is a good source of leads on sublet space that becomes available when offices move or firms break up, which often creates opportunities for reduced rent.

Determine the True Rental Cost

Always ask for the *net* square footage figure from the broker or landlord, and put it into the rental agreement. Divide the monthly or annual rent by net total square footage to get cost per *net* square foot, which is the only true way to measure rent cost for comparison shopping. There can be a 20 percent difference between net square footage and gross square footage, due to poles, beams, corridors, window sills, ducts, stairwells, irregularly shaped premises, etc.

What to Negotiate and Include in Your Rental Agreement

1. Parking for yourself, staff and clients at fixed prices. Don't automatically accept the story that parking is controlled by a separate concessionaire. If pushed, buildings often grant parking as a part of the lease.

2. Access to office at night and on weekends. Will air conditioning, heating and lights be available then at no extra cost? Is building security provided after hours?

3. Is there any furniture from the outgoing tenant you might have?

4. Right of first refusal on additional space in the building if you expand.

5. Air conditioning and heating thermostat controls for your part of the suite.

6. Are electric outlets where you need them? If not, get the landlord to install them.

7. Carpet cleaning or replacement.

8. Painting, replacement, or cleaning of wall coverings.

9. If old drapes can't be cleaned, insist on new ones.

10. Janitorial services such as trash removal, vacuuming, etc., and frequency of service.

11. A one-year term, with two one-year renewal options is best for a starting lawyer. You can stay or move after a one- or two-year experiment.

12. Try to delay the effective date for as long as possible to gain time for delivery of furniture, mailing of announcements, etc., before you have to start paying rent.

13. Don't commit malpractice on yourself before you get your first client. Whether you lease space, share space, or enter into any other arrangement, be sure to *get it in writing* before you move in or spend money on furniture or announcements. Don't depend on a handshake deal.

Start on Announcements

1. Prepare mailing lists.
   a. Law school class (get addresses from alumni association).
   b. Undergraduate classmates (get addresses from alumni association).
   c. High school classmates, if appropriate (get address from alumni association).
   d. Church members, if appropriate.
   e. Family.
   f. Organizations such as sports clubs, social clubs, philanthropic clubs, etc., you belong to (get addresses from club secretary).
   g. Professional associations you belong to.
2. Get sample announcements from printer.
3. Get time and cost estimate from printer.
4. Decide on style, for example, whether to list your principal areas of practice.
5. Order professional cards, and enclose one with each announcement.
6. Use engraved announcements and cards, on good stock.
7. Get cost and time estimate from professional addressing service for addressing, stuffing and mailing.
8. Start addressing the envelopes while the announcements are being printed.
9. Consider buying old postage stamps from a stamp dealer to attract attention to the announcements.

Order Stationery

1. Allow up to two months delivery time for high-quality stationery.
2. Get catalogs with samples.
3. Order letter-size bond letterhead, and second sheets; blank letter-size bond; letter-size envelopes; professional cards; announcements;

paper and covers for wills; billing stationery with window envelopes; and other items suitable to your own practice.

4. Separately buy inexpensive envelopes to use when paying bills.

Get Telephones Ready

1. Estimate number and kind of instruments needed, and number of lines needed by meeting with phone company marketing representative. Don't forget that your secretary, receptionist, and clients will also be using your phones. Consider a second extension in your office for your clients' use.

2. Order equipment, get estimate of waiting time for delivery.

3. Order installation, which may require several days.

4. Reserve telephone number in advance of opening office, so you can give it to printer to put on announcements, cards, and stationery.

5. Consider microwave transmission subscription service if you will have a lot of long-distance calls.

6. Consider yellow page advertising, and listings in directories for other localities.

7. Try to negotiate low cash deposit on telephone equipment.

8. Get an answering service used and recommended by other lawyers or by doctors.

9. Consider getting a cable address (or telex, if you can afford it), if you want to attract international clients.

Order Furnishings

1. By subletting a furnished office you may be able to postpone many of these capital expenses.

2. Determine if major items can be rented instead of being purchased.

3. Determine if used furnishings are available. These cost about 60 percent of the price of new furnishings. Also keep in mind that new furniture often takes from two to six months to deliver.

4. Read ads in local legal newspapers for used furnishings.

5. Minimum furniture for your office:
   a. Picture of family members for desk.
   b. Your desk should be at least 6 feet wide with overhang in front, and treated to protect against scratches and spills.

    c. Your chair. Try it out next to the desk you have selected.

    d. Two to four straight-back chairs.

    e. Wastebasket to match desk.

    f. Clear floor pad for chair if office is carpeted. Don't skimp on pad size, or chair will roll off the edges.

    g. Floor lamp, if additional light is needed.

    h. Potted plant.

    i. Bookshelves.

6. Minimum furnishings for reception room:

    a. Four straight-back chairs.

    b. Magazine rack or table.

    c. Reading light.

    d. Bookshelf.

    e. Coat rack and umbrella stand.

Order Equipment

1. Determine if secretarial service can provide you with dictating equipment as part of its service.

2. Determine if equipment can be rented rather than purchased.

3. Determine if used equipment is available. Should be about 60 percent of new equipment price.

4. Read ads in local newspapers for used equipment and for equipment specials.

5. Minimum equipment:

    a. Secretarial desk, with return for typewriter.

    b. Secretarial chair. If possible, let secretary choose own chair.

    c. Small copy machine, unless one is available nearby.

    d. Dictating equipment including dictating unit, transcription unit and two portable tape recorders, one for your briefcase and one for your car.

    e. Typewriter. Get used if possible, and integrate with word processing equipment.

    f. Word processing equipment. This requires serious study. Don't depend on vendors to advise you. Consult secretaries, office administrators, and other lawyers. Read the publications listed in this book.

    g. Accurate postage scale and postage meter. This will save you considerable money over the years.

Order Office Supplies

1. Get catalogs from several nearby office supply stores.
2. Open charge accounts with these stores. Negotiate for a discount from the list prices in the catalogs.
3. Ask your secretary or another lawyer's secretary to help you make up an initial order list. Consider such items as staplers, paper clips, scissors, two-hole punch, three-hole punch, telephone message pads, rubber stamps with inking pads, scratch pads, legal pads, paper cutter, felt tip markers, staple removers, Scotch tape, desk calendars, pens and pencils, manila envelopes, Rolodex files, coffee maker and cups, check protector, fireproof safe, etc.

Order Insurance

Engage an insurance broker or agent who is likely to refer you business, or buy from several brokers:

1. Malpractice insurance against errors and omissions. Get occurrence rather than claims-made coverage, if possible.
2. General liability insurance.
3. Workers' Compensation insurance.
4. Non-owned automobile insurance.
5. File replacement and valuable papers coverage.
6. Fire and theft insurance, for replacement value.
7. Get "umbrella" coverage, if available.
8. Check with broker or bank for financing of premiums through monthly payments.
9. Check if "office block" policy available.

Start Secretarial and Nonlawyer Hiring

1. Adopt a personnel manual. A checklist of the topics to cover appears in *The Lawyer's Handbook* (rev. ed. 1978), available from ICLE, Hutchins Hall, Ann Arbor, MI 48109, for $45.00.
2. Check with local high schools, junior colleges, business colleges and universities for trainee secretarial and clerical help who will work without pay or for low pay to get work training credits. Excellent source of capable trainees.
3. Get "Secretarial Hiring Kits," to test basic skills, for example, from E.F. Wunderlich & Associates, Inc., P.O. Box 7, Northfield,

IL 60093, or from Law Research Institute, 220 South 200 East, Suite 320, Salt Lake City, UT 84111.

4. Adopt *A Style Manual for the Law Office,* available from Order Fulfillment, ABA Economics of Law Practice Section, 750 N. Lake Shore Drive, Chicago, IL 60611, for $15.00 ($10.00 to Section members).

5. Find out what monographs or other publications are available from the American Bar Association Economics of Law Practice Section. New monographs are continually being published.

6. Allow three weeks for advertising and interviewing of applicants, and an additional two weeks notice which the successful candidate may have to give his or her present employer.

Start a Filing System

1. Get help from a legal secretary or office administrator in setting up a filing system. The file folders are just part of the system.

2. Allow six to eight weeks for delivery of supplies.

3. Install a numerical system rather than an alphabetical system, using vertical rather than horizontal files. Various systems are suggested in the publications listed below.

Start an Accounting System

1. Engage a CPA to be your accountant. Have the accountant install a system for bookkeeping and for timekeeping, and order accounting supplies for you.

2. If you choose not to use a CPA, review the systems suggested in the publications listed below, and adopt a system appropriate to your practice.

3. Consider contracting with a service bureau for timekeeping and billing.

4. Again, contact the American Bar Association Economics of Law Practice Section for appropriate publications.

Prepare Budgets

1. Get help from a CPA in preparing budget statements that can be used in applying for loans or credit from a bank.

2. A practice cash budget should be prepared for the first year, by month, estimating your expenses. Include such items as rent, telephone, insurance, furnishings and equipment, copy equipment charges, sta-

tionery, office supplies, bar dues (including lawyer reference service fees), legal newspapers, attorney service, salaries, announcements (including postage and addressing), continuing education seminars and programs, diploma framing, automobile, parking (if not included in rent), estimates of costs to be advanced, and business development (lunches, entertainment, etc.).

3. A personal living expense cash budget should also be prepared by month for your first year. Allow money for some recreation and for medical expenses.

4. To cover these expenses, consider:
   a. Estimated income from fees for services.
   b. Savings accounts.
   c. Working spouse.
   d. Relatives who may offer help.
   e. Bank loan.
   f. SBA guaranteed loan.
   g. Credit union loan.
   h. Bar association credit union loan.

Licenses, Permits, etc.

1. Obtain federal employer identification number.
2. File federal quarterly income tax estimates for personal income taxes.
3. Obtain city or county licenses or permits, as required.
4. Notify state bar of address.
5. Join local bar association.
6. Join Young Lawyers Association or Section of your state bar.
7. Join lawyer reference services.
8. Notify possible sources of court-appointed work of your availability.

Open Bank Accounts

1. Open office account and get checks printed.
2. Open client trust account and get checks printed.
3. Open credit line with banker.
4. Arrange for safe deposit box for wills and other client valuables.

Buy Only Essential Library Items

A library is a bottomless pit, which should be avoided during the first year of practice to the extent possible. Unannotated codes and some legal journals are probably essential. Use other libraries, at least at the start. Don't try to build your own until you can afford it.

Where to Get More Answers

Every law office should have the publications listed below as its basic reference library for management suggestions. In this basic library you will find the solution to almost any problem you will have to face. This entire library can probably be obtained for less than $100.00 and this may be the best investment in your practice you can make

1. *Opening a Law Office* (1976) by The California Young Lawyers Association of the State Bar of California, 555 Franklin Street, San Francisco, CA 94102. A comprehensive California-oriented summary. 53 pages. $3.00.

2. *How to Operate an Efficient Law Office* (1976), by Paul N. Luvera, Jr., P.O. Box 427, Mount Vernon, WA 98273. Excellent manual for organizing a small office. 85 pages. Available from the author. $10.00

3. *The Thrifty Fifty* (1979), by James E. Brill, P.O. Box 22870, Houston, TX 77027. A fantastic source of tips for in-house systems and procedures for a law office. Should be read by all non-lawyers in office, as well as lawyers. 31 pages. Available free from the author.

4. *Practicing Law Profitably* (8th ed, 1979), by Kline D. Strong, 1039 Vista View Drive, Salt Lake City, UT 84108. A compendium of suggestions, encompassing whole systems. Also covers some conceptual areas. Excellent reference book for problems in specific areas. 407 pages. Available from the author. $5.00.

5. *The Lawyer's Handbook,* available from ICLE, Hutchins Hall, Ann Arbor, MI 48109. Covers several areas of practice management. 463 pages. $45.00.

6. *Legal Economics,* bi-monthly publication of ABA Economics of Law Practice Section, 750 N. Lake Shore Drive, Chicago, IL 60611. Buy all back issues available and subscribe currently. Almost any problem you have can be found in one issue or another. Section dues of $17.50 per year includes subscription to this publication. You must be an ABA member to join the Section.

7. Various monographs, including *Model Accounting System, How to Create-A-System for the Law Office, Style Manual, Management Controls, Word Processing Equipment,* etc., available from the ABA Economics of Law Practice Section. You need not be a Section member to order these materials. Ask for the Section catalog (750 N. Lake Shore Drive, Chicago, IL 60611).

8. Articles by J. Nick De Meo of Santa Rosa, California, in back issues of the *California State Bar Journal.* Mr. De Meo has created whole systems in different areas of practice management.

9. Articles by J. Harris Morgan of Dallas, Texas, in back issues of *Texas Bar Journal.* In my opinion, J. Harris Morgan is the greatest mind and personality in the management of a law office and practice.

10. *The Bottom Line,* publication of the Economics of Law Practice Section of the State Bar of California.

Keep Up with New Developments

The least expensive and most comprehensive way to keep current in this field is by belonging to the Economics of Law Practice Sections of the American Bar Association and of your state bar. For further information, write to: Economics of Law Practice Section, American Bar Association, 750 N. Lake Shore Drive, Chicago, IL 60611.

Index

Join the Law Student Division of the ABA

APPLICATION

Name _____
       Last   First   Middle

Street _____ City _____ State _____ Zip _____

Law School _____ City _____

Birth Date			Law School Entry		Prospective Graduation Date	
Month	Day	Year	Month	Year	Month	Year

As a law student member of the ABA, I will abide by its Constitution and By-Laws.

Signature _____ Date _____

☐ Enclosed is my membership fee, which includes an allocation of $2.75 for the *ABA Journal* and $2.50 for the *Student Lawyer:* $10.00 after August 31, 1984; $8.00 until August 31, 1984.

☐ Enclosed is $3.00 more for membership in the Section of Economics of Law Practice.

Send check and application to:
Member Records, ABA, 1155 E. 60th St., Chicago, IL 60637

Office Use Only:	☐ ☐	☐ ☐	☐ ☐
	NUMERIC STATE CODE	ALPHA STATE CODE	LAW SCHOOL CODE

Other Books from the Section of Economics of Law Practice

SYSTEMS

Docket Control Systems for Lawyers. The most effective means to avoid malpractice claims is a strict docket control system. This manual will help you implement a monitoring system in your law office.

How to Create-a-System for the Law Office. This manual will help you create systems for collections, divorces, incorporations, adoptions, personal injury litigation, and many other common legal tasks.

Retrieval Systems for Lawyers. This guide will introduce you to techniques for preserving research and retrieving it for use with new clients.

Style Manual. Standardize the form, content, arrangement, and style of your legal documents using this manual.

Model Accounting System. This guide will show you how to systematize your accounting procedures, and it will enable you to control and to compare income and expenses professionally.

The Lawyer's Handbook. More than 100,000 lawyers have used the *Handbook* to help streamline their office systems. Updated annually.

Simplified Accounting Systems and Concepts for Lawyers. This book explains and illustrates effective bookkeeping systems for the smaller firm, and offers a standard chart of accounts.

Management of a Family Law Practice. In this book you'll find procedures for systematizing a divorce practice, minimizing collection problems, and introducing clients to your services.

EQUIPMENT AND TECHNOLOGY

Choosing and Using Computers. Includes critical information for small firms on microcomputer hardware and software.

LOCATE. This directory contains listings of vendors supplying legal software.

Word Processing Equipment. This basic guide will help you understand the basic operation of automatic typewriters, and help you evaluate your unique office needs.

Planning for Computers. Intended for medium and large firms wishing to evaluate their data processing needs.

Telephone Equipment for the Law Office. This is an introduction to the telephone and facsimile systems available to the law office.

ALSO AVAILABLE

Flying Solo. This book is a collection of 48 articles, written by solo practitioners. Discusses major aspects of starting, managing, and maintaining a successful solo practice.

Expanding Your Law Practice: The Ethical Risks. This book points out the principal ethical issues and the way courts, disciplinary agencies, and ethics advisory committees have dealt with public relations, the operation of multiple office law firms, and dual professional practice and joint ventures with nonlawyers.

Nonlegal Careers for Lawyers in the Private Sector. This book identifies the pros and cons of a nonlegal career in the private sector. It discusses where you can find the most appealing jobs, and how to choose the right one for you.

Your New Lawyer. This is a complete legal employer's guide to recruitment, development, and management of new lawyers.

Legal Fees and Representation Agreements. Includes easy-to-use models for written client/lawyer and counsel/associated counsel agreements.

Law Office Staff Manual. Model policies and procedures for the general administration of the law office.

Model Partnership Agreement. A partnership agreement focusing on the needs of an office with two to ten lawyers.

Working with Legal Assistants. This is a two-volume set containing systems, techniques, and ideas for using legal assistants.

How to Avoid Being Sued by Your Client. Describes numerous areas of potential liability, discusses preventive measures, and analyzes special insurance coverage.

The Best of Legal Economics. Contains 46 articles on law office management gleaned from the Section's bimonthly magazine.

How to Start and Build a Law Practice. Now in its fifth printing, this classic book will give you advice on building a successful law practice.

New Tricks for Old Dogs. This book contains numerous tips from practicing attorneys for solving a variety of problems.

Cost Accounting for Law Firms

Financial Management of Law Firms

Management Controls and Reporting

Profit Planning and Budgeting for Law Firms

These four books in the financial management monograph series will help attorneys manage the financial aspects of their practice.

Law Office Organization. This is the classic work on the subject, written by Reginald Heber Smith.

ORDER FORM

Quantity	Title	ELP† Section Price	Regular Price	Total
_____	Best of Legal Economics (5110053)	$20.00	$25.00	$ _____
_____	Choosing and Using Computers (5110076)	28.00	38.00	_____
_____	Cost Accounting for Law Firms (5110088)	15.00	25.00	_____
_____	Docket Control Systems (5110063)	12.00	22.00	_____
_____	Expanding Your Law Practice: The Ethical Risks (5110090)	14.95	19.95	_____
_____	Financial Management Monograph Series--4-volume set (5110089)	49.95	79.95	_____
_____	Financial Management of Law Firms (5110045)	15.00	25.00	_____
_____	Flying Solo (5110084)	34.95	39.95	_____
_____	How to Avoid Being Sued (5110068)	11.00	20.00	_____
	How to Create-A-System for the Law Office			
_____	(5110027—without cassette)	20.00	25.00	_____
_____	(5110028—with cassette)	25.00	30.00	_____
_____	How to Start and Build a Law Practice (5110080)	9.95‡	14.95	_____
_____	Law Office Organization (5110079)	10.00	15.00	_____
_____	Law Office Staff Manual (5110071)	18.00	28.00	_____
_____	Lawyer's Handbook	*	*	_____
_____	Legal Fees and Representation Agreements (5110074)	11.00	20.00	_____
_____	LOCATE (5110085)	18.00	28.00	_____
_____	Management Controls (5110049)	15.00	25.00	_____
_____	Management of a Family Law Practice (5110066)	20.00	20.00	_____
_____	Model Accounting System (5110039)	15.00	25.00	_____
_____	Model Partnership Agreement (5110072)	10.00	15.00	_____
_____	New Tricks for Old Dogs (5110048)	10.00	15.00	_____
_____	Nonlegal Careers: In the Private Sector (5110082)	9.95	14.95	_____
_____	Planning for Computers (5110067)	13.00	25.00	_____
_____	Profit Planning and Budgeting (5110056)	15.00	25.00	_____
_____	Retrieval Systems (5110057)	12.00	22.00	_____
_____	Simplified Accounting Systems (5110073)	24.00	34.00	_____
_____	Style Manual (5110042)	10.00	15.00	_____
_____	Telephone Equipment (5110077)	17.00	25.00	_____
_____	Word Processing Equipment (5110051)	10.00	20.00	_____
	Working with Legal Assistants			
_____	Volume 1 (5110060)	25.00	25.00	_____
_____	Volume 2 (5110064)	40.00	40.00	_____
_____	Volumes 1 & 2 (5110065)	55.00	55.00	_____
_____	Your New Lawyer (5110075)	35.00	45.00	_____

†Economics of Law Practice.

‡Also includes members of the Law Student Division.

*The hardbound edition of *The Lawyer's Handbook* ($50.00) may be ordered from Book Dept., ICLE, Hutchins Hall, Ann Arbor, MI 48109. Also inquire about *Law Office Information Service* (LOIS), a comprehensive bibliography on law firm management.

**You must be an ABA member to join the Section. Annual dues are: $17.50, or $3.00 for Law Student Division members.

Handling Charge _____ $2.00

ELP Membership** _____

TOTAL $ _____

☐ Check/money order payable to American Bar Association enclosed.　　☐ MasterCard　　☐ Visa

Credit Card Number _____　　Exp. Date _____

Signature _____

Name _____

Firm or Company _____

Address _____

City _____　State _____　Zip _____

IMPORTANT: A phone number will speed your order if we need to contact you: _____

Allow four to six weeks for delivery.

Please send payment to: **American Bar Association, Order Fulfillment 511, 750 N. Lake Shore Drive, Chicago, Illinois 60611.**